SRI AUROBINDO

OR

THE POETICS OF *Hope*

SRI AUROBINDO
OR
THE POETICS OF *Hope*

MURALI SIVARAMAKRISHNAN

AUTHORSPRESS

Worldwide Circulation through Authorspress Global Network
First Published in 2022
by
Authorspress
Q-2A Hauz Khas Enclave, New Delhi-110 016 (India)
Phone: (0) 9818049852
E-mail: authorspressgroup@gmail.com
Website: www.authorspressbooks.com

Sri Aurobindo or the Poetics of Hope
ISBN 978-93-5529-050-2

Printed in India at Kensington Press

For
Appa and Amma

Contents

1. Sri Aurobindo or the Poetics of Hope 9
2. The Inner Fields: Poetry and the Triple Transformation 14
3. Prakriti and the Manifestations of Spiritual Consciousness: Dimensions of Nature and the Vedic Lineage of an Eco-Discourse in Sri Aurobindo's *Savitri* 28
4. *Savitri* – Mahakavya 53
5. Being and Becoming: The Premises of Sri Aurobindo's Aesthetics 72
6. Conceptualising Poetic Futures: Visions and Variations 99
7. On Reading Sri Aurobindo: Blindness, Insight, Outlook and a Perspective 117

Appendices 132

Index 155

CHAPTER 1

Sri Aurobindo or the Poetics of Hope

This is indeed a time for introspection--even for the common man and woman. Our ubiquitous social media is flooded with quips, quotes, citations and aphorisms reflecting upon, exploring and explaining life. However, philosophers and mystics, scholars and poets, have always and at all times, been struggling with such fundamental questions of existence in profound seriousness. The inner quest for meaning has perhaps created a graph toward a perennial philosophy. And of course only the ardent and the inquisitive mind have been able to trace this graph of hope. The journey toward the interior spaces leads the seeker into the lesser trod dimensions of spirituality, but once initiated into these levels, the genuine inquirer is certain to meet with innumerable like-minded seekers. Sri Aurobindo (1872-1950) was ceaseless in his inner search; for him self-reflexivity came naturally.

This book deals with Sri Aurobindo's philosophy and poetics – both intricately connected. It is a spiritual aesthetic that he proposes. The chapters in this book argue that Sri Aurobindo's spirituality needs to be seen in a global perspective; it was as much part of his social and political consciousness as it was of his religious, His ceaseless endeavour to view life in its totality, and to see it whole, signifies the most outstanding fact about his spiritual standpoint. Right from his earliest contact with the Indian situation which came only as a second phase after his exposure to Europe, Sri Aurobindo – born as Aurobindo Ghose – was convinced of the legitimacy of an integral awareness. And what he came to identify as the two negations – the materialist's denial of an eternal Being behind the phenomenal and the ascetic's refusal to accept the reality of the world – were as he saw it the two major impediments in the way towards a comprehensive awareness and affirmation in the history of human thought, and a new and rich self-fulfilment in an integral existence for the individual and the humankind alike. He sought to integrate life and spirit into a cosmic whole and to embody the unified vision in an ascent to Gnostic humanity. This call towards an integral attitude might also be traced to the apparently contradictory nature of his historical situation.

Born in India and brought up in England, the prophet of militant nationalism and the silent recluse of Pondicherry, the Yogi of the ancient Vedic temperament and the author of a prodigious variety of writings in the English language ranging from songs and sonnets to narratives and epics, from political pamphlets to philosophical treatises, he combined in himself both the West and the East. To understand his philosophy and thereby appraise his aesthetic theories which are organically unified with his philosophical insight, we have to take into account the impact of both the West and the East-the "Indian impact" because Sri Aurobindo deliberately chose to be an Indian.

Sri Aurobindo was born on 15th August, 1872, in Calcutta, as *Aurobindo Ackroyd Ghose*, the third son of Krishnadhan Ghose and Swarnalata Devi. It was a time when hundreds of years of stupor and languor permeated by inner conflicts and turbulations in the Indian scene had resulted in the consolidation of British colonialism, and concurrent to it, a new upsurge of national ethos was in the process of crystallising. But he confronted the question of what it meant to be an Indian only much later, when he returned from England, a fiery young man of twenty-one, seasoned in European classical learning, well-versed in Greek and Latin, and eminently ratiocinative. His early writings in the *Bandemataram* and the *Karmayogin* about India and her heritage were more of a justification for his national identity of which he was only slowly becoming aware, and a violent reaction against the colonised experience. But later, as his politics took him deeper and deeper into the very heart of nationalism, and his reading revealed to him the essence of Indian wisdom, he, despite the inner pressure in him to identify with what was a partisan view, chose an integral cosmic stance. This is what makes Sri Aurobindo, as Mokashi Punekar has said, "a unique phenomenon." For, "He is not a mere product of the *Hindu resurgence*; he brought to it a creative continuity with European thought."

Everything that he wrote argues not merely for the integral conservation of higher values of existence, but also for a progressive increase of the levels of being, and the increasing progression calls for a new heaven and a new earth. Similarly there is evidenced a radical difference in his later mature writings as they are naturally the products of a qualitatively higher order than the earlier work. However, there does endure a discernible design for a massive visionary and critical structure in Sri Aurobindo's earlier writings to be constantly and periodically modified and developed later. He was never a systematic philosopher though. His writings bear testimony but to his deep-felt inner experiences. They embody the essentially poetic vision of a Rishi, seer-poet. His aesthetics is inherently implied in the creative experience of reality and not an aesthetic theory that is inferred intellectually and systematically. Hardly can it be said of any other poet or philosopher as can be said of him that they lived their poetic visions.

In sheer bulk and variety of subjects his creative output is stupendous: apart from translations from Sanskrit, Greek and other languages, social and political writings, philosophical treatises, speculations on the Veda, Upanishad and the Gita and massive volumes on Yoga, his work includes two epics and some two hundred odd poems. He undertook all this without any appeal for public recognition, literary acceptance or social status. A quiet man with a serious disposition and an intense passion for literature and thought, Sri Aurobindo was, as Romain Rolland chose to describe him, "the most noble representative of the Neo-Vedantic spirit… the foremost of Indian thinkers," and also, "the completest synthesis that has been realised to this day of the genius of Asia and the genius of Europe," and the last of the great Rishis who held in his hand "in firm and unrelaxed grip, the bow of creative energy." Anyone who came into the circle of this creative personality experienced a strange mystic rapture, the extreme form of which Dilip Kumar Roy noted:

> I can only say that in his presence I felt myself gripped by a silent wonder and intense longing to lay my utter self at his feet and lie cradled in his indefinable Grace.

Variously compared with Hegel, Bergson, Bradley and Heidegger and classed with Radhakrishnan as a notable philosopher, with Gandhi and Tagore as a leader of modern India, and ranked with Sri Ramakrishna and Maharshi Ramana as a saint, Sri Aurobindo's life falls into three distinct phases. At the age of seven he was taken to England and with his coming back to India in 1893 the first European phase ends and the political one begins. Seventeen years of militant nationalistic activities landed him in jail where the most significant experience of his life occurred – a mystic vision of

Krishna-which brought in an entirely new dimension to his life and work. Although this event marks a turning point in his life and the beginning of its third phase, the earlier experiences were but preparatory to this. The developing life of a true mystic traces a gradual ascent in the scale of experience and values; Sri Aurobindo's life is rich and complete in its many-sided development and follows a clear pattern of ascent and integration. From the Cambridge scholar through the militant patriot to the silent Yogi of Pondicherry it delineates a qualitative transformation, integrating everything which has gone before into a higher plane of consciousness.

With Sri Aurobindo the conventional division of the outer and inner world, subjective and objective reality, is no longer meaningful. To him action was the essence of life but it did not mean a turbulent agitation on the physical plane; it was an action that came by a conscious subjection and merging of the ego in the divine Self, a liberating action. "When we strive to act, the forces of nature do their will with us," Sri Aurobindo explains in an early article, "when we grow still, we become their master… The more complete the calm… the greater the force in action." To the man whose intellect is delivered from the enslavement to dualities, from the oppositions of inner and outer, silence is the superior action – the accent is on "being" rather than "doing." Thus the "action" of the "superior man" often stands apart in a clear variance from the ordinary.

And as a man who "knew." Sri Aurobindo left politics as suddenly and unceremoniously as he had come in. For a writer in whom the man and the work are necessarily one, this transformation from the militant political activist to the self-exiled recluse calls for closer attention.

Sri Aurobindo passed thirteen years, from 1893 to 1906, at Baroda working in various government departments and later teaching French and English in the Baroda College. These were years of self-culture, literary activity and secret political engagements. He studied Sanskrit and other Indian languages, assimilated the spirit of Indian culture and civilisation, and in 1904 began practicing Yoga, starting with pranayama as explained to him by a friend, a disciple of Brahmananda. There was, as he found, no conflict or wavering between Yoga and politics – when he started Yoga he carried on both without any idea of opposition between them. In 1908 he met Vishnu Bhaskar Lele of Gwalior, who advanced him further in Yoga giving him a greater insight, strength and faith, and more confidence in himself. By this time he had left Baroda and taken up the position of the Principal of the newly founded Bengal National College in Calcutta. Then on till 1907 when he was arrested for sedition and later acquitted, he wrote and spoke for a new national awareness, preached a militant activism and meditated on God and man. The Bandemataram, the newspaper and weekly that he jointly edited with Bepin Chandra Pal, carries the bulk of his early political pamphleteering prior to being prosecuted; the Karmayogin and the Dharma, in English and in Bengali repectively, which he edited single-handedly, following his acquittal, sound a markedly different tone from these early rebellious incitements – they reveal the workings of a mind and an inner spiritual energy pressing upon it for an exclusive concentration. In a speech delivered at Uttarpara on May 30, 1909, published in the Karmayogin, he gave utterance to his remarkable spiritual experiences in the Alipore jail. As the walls of materiality crumbled around him revealing the omnipresence of Krishna, Sri Aurobindo underwent an experiential conviction of all that he had earlier gathered intellectually from his readings of the Gita, the Upanishads and the Vedas.

This experience convinced him of the fact that all beings are united in One Self, but divided by a certain separateness of consciousness, an ignorance of their true self. He found that it was possible through certain psychological disciplines to remove this veil of separating consciousness and become aware of the true Being, the Divinity within and without. In Yoga, Sri Aurobindo found a means of inward living and transformation.

In Sri Aurobindo's vision the theoretical is bound up with the practical – gnosis and praxis – the metaphysical is integrated with the psychological. His philosophy is not an abstract theoretical system but a concise register of his experiences, and his finding that certain mantras of the Rig Veda substantially corroborated his own experiences strengthened his conviction of their validity.

The book explores the philosophy and poetics of Sri Aurobindo.

CHAPTER 2

The Inner Fields: Poetry and the Triple Transformation

The whole of my life
Summed up in these words
I used to be raw
Then I was cooked
Now... on fire.

– Jalal ud din Rumi

I wrote the following some time ago before the pandemic crisis. I had then written with the hope that the political, social, environmental and spiritual crises that the globalising forces of market economy had unleashed could be countered with a transformation of internal perspective, a call toward the deeper spiritual self. I wrote with the fervent hope that the prophet of Life Divine had perceived the spiritual at the heart of all, and his call needed heeding in troubled times. Poetry could be salve, poetry could be reclamation, and poetry could call our wayward selves to order and a future. I believe the hope and the prayer still stands, and hence what I had written then appears still relevant in troubled times like these.

Perhaps, there is hardly any relevance to poetry in the present day world at the outside; there is even less relevance to discussing religion in the contemporary context in the face of intolerance and terrorism and market values. When Rumi, whom I have quoted at the beginning, was alive and writing about his inner transformation, as several insightful scholars have pointed out, the Islamic world was on the gruesome rampage elsewhere; and yet one cannot casually dismiss him as having been neither apolitical nor insensitive to worldly issues, if one were to take the pains to read him between the lines. Perhaps, the genuine poet across cultures is often condemned to bear witness to humanity's horrible deeds and remain singing in isolation, poetically "*on fire*" Or perhaps apparently turn his/her back on what others hold as life and seek the profounder truths of being and becoming – an interior transformation?

The situation in India today warrants lesser significance for the finer poetic sensibilities either. And as the idea of religion in its fundamentalist avatar ever weaves a fabric of terror and violence rather than what basically all religions teach – tolerance and love – what then is the relevance of raking up the dream boat of a poet-mystic who lived and wrote in the last century about life divine and about divinising one's life in its totality? In brief what does the work of Sri Aurobindo entail? Can it reach beyond the centuries and speak to us in the present like the poetry of Rumi albeit in a different context? Will it appeal to the sensibility of the new generation like say a Paulo Coelho or a Jostein Gaarder? It might be that the work of Sri Aurobindo may not be easy to absorb like that of the verse of Rumi or Kabir. Its prodigious philosophical burden might hamper its easy digestion. But then, however, in our pursuit of existence we need to bring to bear genuine commitment and a deeper sincerity, and certainly a little extra effort would lead us an extra mile in understanding and perhaps an inch closer to truth. Saints and scholars, poets and mystics, all have lived their lives intensely; otherwise they would not have become what they became.

These are days when we boast of information at our fingertips, and technology has helped to throw the entire world flat on its surface for us to read and browse like an open book. And yet if we hold within ourselves the desire to know more we need to necessarily take that extra effort. No saint or rishi who has walked the earth in flesh and blood has left without leaving his/her clear footprints for us to trace. Well, even their dreams could catch fire in the process of life's cooking.

Behind Sri Aurobindo's philosophical speculation lie years of systematic exploration of the esoteric dimensions of Vedic poetry and Vedantic thought, and an interior transformation through the methodology of yoga. His entire life was a constant pursuit of deeper levels of existence. And he followed it with a will and a purpose. In his systematic philosophical explication Sri Aurobindo traces the ascent of consciousness through what the Vedantic thought distinguishes as levels of the material, the vital, the mental, and the ideal, the spiritual or beatific. And as he argues with the aid of a spiritual logic, there are grades and ranges of consciousness subconscient and superconscient to our everyday waking consciousness. (See *The Life Divine*, p 260) In his scheme of things, almost all our actions in the world are done in the domain of the

Ignorance, where a separatist ego exists and divides our true selves from the spiritual. Probably this awareness is the reason why the spiritual call took precedence above all else in his life. At the outside he simply dropped politics and withdrew into the silence and solitude of Pondicherry.

The *Life Divine* is a substantial explication of his philosophy of being and becoming, integrating the yoga sutras and the Vedic vision. Because of the vastness of its canvas and the complexity of its argument the entire book does not yield to any shortening or condensed version; we can but take short sorties into it and construct an angle of perception that allows us to share his vision of spiritual becoming. Self-knowledge, as he points out, is impossible unless we go behind our surface existence, (223) and in his specialised terminology, it is the *soul*, that is the seat of essential aesthetic relish, and this constitutes the aesthetic being in humans, "receptive to the joy of the variety of existence" (ibid) In resorting to this deeper spiritual being we can relish the essential joy of existence, and thus Aurobindian aesthetics is an aesthesis of spiritual being and Godward becoming. The point that marks him off from several other mystics is his analytical thinking and imaginative writing that ran on parallel rails throughout his life. He made a "religion" of poetry just like some of the British Romantic poets did, but as different from them he was a systematic philosopher and a practicing yogi. From political thought, through yoga and mysticism, we can trace his transformation. In what follows my attempt would be to seek simple parallels between Sri Aurobindo's own short poems and what he designates as the transformation of being. Of course a poet need not follow a pre-planned course explaining or ratifying his/her system of belief; and Sri Aurobindo was not a propagandist either. So then one cannot try and harness his poetic voice in a linear order of explication, for as he rightly says, *vision is the characteristic power of the poet*, and vision does not follow logic or reason. Nevertheless, let us make a simple foray into his domain of experience and seek for correspondences and clarifications.

Sri Aurobindo's opening thesis is that *all problems of existence are essentially problems of harmony,* and thus to seek for harmony with nature and beyond that with the essential spirit is the natural inclination of the thinking self. When there is a rupture or imbalance with *prakriti* it is often the innate spiritual being in the human self that sets the human aspirant on the right course for the pursuit of his/her true being and a resultant transformation. As long as we allow ourselves to be led by the Inconscient and the Ignorance, we will live in the domain of duality, evil, pain, and falsehood. *It would follow that there can be no final solution until we have turned our inconscience into the greater consciousness, made the truth of self and spirit our life basis and transformed our ignorance into higher knowledge.... A complete and radical transformation of our nature is the only true solution.* (627)

And from this false and evil-ridden world of dualities we need to turn to our spiritual selves for the transformation. *Purification of the nature by the "influence" of the Spirit is now what I mean by transformation.* (SABCL XXII 115-16) And according to him there is this triple transformation that needs to take place.

The first step of self-realisation is to enthrone the soul, the divine psychic individual in the place of the ego. Take a look at this sonnet "The Inner Fields"

> There is a brighter ether than this blue
> Pretence of an enveloping heavenly vault,
> A deeper greenness than this laughing assault
> Of emerald rapture pearled with tears of dew.
> Immortal spaces of cerulean hue
> Are in our reach and fields without this fault
> Of drab brown earth and streams that never halt
> In their deep murmur which white flowers strew
>
> Floating like stars upon a strip of sky.
> This world behind is made of truer stuff
> Than the manufactured tissue of earth's grace.
> There we can walk and see the gods go by
> And sip from Hebe's cup nectar enough
> To make for us heavenly limbs and deathless face.

There is much more than what meets the eye, ear and touch – this is what the poem states. At the very outset the sonnet reveals the structural transformation after one realises the profundity of deeper experiences behind the apparent and phenomenal world – this is done through the sestet standing separate from the octet. In the first stanza there is a loudness of colour and sense, of gravity and touch, while in the second there is a certain non-materiality, in terms of a floating in space not governed by the gravity of earth or phenomena. This sense experience of a-sensual noumena is what this poem is generally about. This is where we take our first preliminary step to self-realisation. Of course there is no substantial conclusion: the poet appears to leave us all of a sudden with a gentle nudge toward "the world behind" what we had so far held as real. Perhaps on account of its structure the poem is intended to effect just that: *Floating like stars upon a strip of sky….*

Anyway there is the inception of a new sense in terms of a poetics of perception that the reader is invited to share. From here to the larger engaging vision of a multitude of earths the distance is not too far.

The Other Earths

An irised multitude of hills and seas,
And glint of brooks in the green wilderness,
And trackless stars, and miracled symphonies
Of hues that float in ethers shadowless,
A dance of fire-flies in the fretted gloom,
In a pale midnight the moon's silver flare,
Fire-importunities of scarlet bloom
And bright suddenness of wings in a golden air,

Strange bird and animal forms like memories cast
On the rapt silence of unearthly woods,
Calm faces of the gods on backgrounds vast
Bringing the marvel of the infinitudes,
Through glimmering veils of wonder and delight
World after world bursts on the awakened sight.

Even in a sort of preliminary reading one can note the tonal difference between the two sonnets. While the previous one appears to state some experience that is there, and can be had, (*there is a certain experience which could be within our reach*) the second one bursts directly on to the experience *per se*. The subject who undergoes this experience does not even appear until the last line and that too almost as a sort of afterthought! There is no ego here only the expansion of vision and insight, *bursting on the awakened sight.*

Some scholars would insist on a sort of linear analysis of Sri Aurobindo's works, whereby one unfolds his conceptual and aesthetic framework in a systematic and chronological manner. Such an analysis would perhaps follow the time scale of these poetic compositions: when it was composed, the spiritual levels he had achieved at that specific time, and the corresponding corroborations evinced by his philosophical and explicatory epistles written to various disciples etc. Of course this could yield suitable results no doubt. But in what follows my own methodology would be to contextualise the poetic pieces primarily in terms of their poetic visions that they afford irrespective of whether they are juvenilia or verses composed at a later stage in the yogi's life. What I would thus look for would be poetic evidences that dovetail with spiritual experiences. It would do well if one were to keep in mind the idea that poetic experiences in themselves do not follow any time scale or logical structure: they occur at random and in the case of a yogi poet sometimes visions could be etched in a poetic mould much before or after they surface to the logical mind.

The two sonnets arranged side by side appear to complete a totality of vision and insight. One speaks of the possibilities the other carries it forward. The reader is invited to share. What is significant for us here is that Sri Aurobindo's works function as open texts allowing for the willing reader to explore and make connections wherever possible. They cannot be dismissed as mere pieces of a large jigsaw puzzle. They are attempts to gather together bits and pieces of the inner experience of the touch of the spirit and the awakening of the soul. There are certainly other instances in the poems where this specific experience of the opening up of the aesthetic being is evident. At almost no point in his spiritual evolution has the poet ceased to explore correspondence through poetic utterance.

The next step in spiritual becoming is to become aware of the eternal self in us unborn and one with the self of all beings. This self-realisation liberates and universalises. As we read in the following sonnet: *The Soul of all that lives, calm, pure, alone,/Revealed its boundless self, mystic and bare.* In the structure of this line we can encounter the transformation of vision. The soul of all beings lives, calm and pure and alone. Despite its essential passive nature the soul is able to reveal itself in its boundless, mystic and bare aloneness. The sensing self on the other hand assumes a passive role receiving the enlargement of vision.

The Hill-top Temple

After unnumbered steps of a hill-stair
I saw upon earth's head brilliant with sun
The immobile Goddess in her house of stone
In a loneliness of meditating air.
Wise were the human hands that set her there
Above the world and Time's dominion;
The Soul of all that lives, calm, pure, alone,
Revealed its boundless self-mystic and bare.

Our body is an epitome of some Vast
That masks its presence by our humanness.
In us the secret Spirit can indite
A page and summary of the Infinite,
A nodus of Eternity expressed
Live in an image and a sculptured face.

Now, the next sonnet that follows however, does enfold any unified receiving eye and self. The narrative here revolves round the duality of "*my*-self" and "thy-self."

Divine Sight

Each sight is now immortal with Thy bliss:
My soul through the rapt eyes has come to see;
A veil is rent and they no more can miss
The miracle of Thy world-epiphany.
Into an ecstasy of vision caught
Each natural object is of Thee a part,
A rapture-symbol from Thy substance wrought,
A poem shaped in Beauty's living heart,

A master-work of colour and design,
A mighty sweetness borne on grandeur's wings;
A burdened wonder of significant line
Reveals itself in even commonest things.
All forms are Thy dream-dialect of delight,
O Absolute, O vivid Infinite.

The key lines in this piece are: *A burdened wonder of significant line/Reveals itself in even commonest things.* With the touch of the divine soul even the ordinary things appear uncommon in *burdened wonder*! The word burden here is to be interpreted creatively as the self's quality in still being able to establish a connection to the earth, to mortality, to transience. There is the gravity of reality, the material status of the earth. And yet they appear in sweetness and delight, the *ananda* of existence, felt in the veins and gathered in the soul: sat-chit-ananda. The gradual increase of awareness is modified in the octet and sestet; while in the first eight lines we encounter a spate of evanescent imagery like these:

The miracle of Thy world-epiphany.
Into an ecstasy of vision caught
Each natural object is of Thee a part,
A rapture-symbol from Thy substance wrought,
A poem shaped in Beauty's living heart...

The sestet on the other hand marks a clear break with its *burdened wonder of significant line revealing itself in even commonest things!* Words like *master-work, mighty sweetness, burdened wonder* are such almost ordinary ones that could evoke everyday feelings but infused with some extraordinary energy, because:

All forms are Thy dream-dialect of delight,
O Absolute, O vivid Infinite.

Life has multiple levels of being and having, knowing and becoming. Once the transcendental is felt within and the soul realises the deep calm even the ordinary is infused with the extraordinary.

The third step is to know the Divine Being who is at once our supreme transcendent Self, the Cosmic Being, foundation of our universality … (*The Life Divine,* 631)

In a poem entitled The Witness and the Wheel, the poet writes:

Witness, who then art thou, one with thee who am I,
Nameless, watching the Wheel whirl across Time and Space?

There is a divinity that sits in the centre of all existence and watches, witnessing all action. This is our transcendent Self, our cosmic self. In the *Mundaka Upanishad III, 1)* we can read:

Dva suparna sayuja sakhaya samanam vrksam parisavajate
Tayor anyah pippalam svadv atty anasnann anyobhicskasiti

Two birds, companions (who are) always united, cling to the self-same tree. Of these two, the one eats the sweet fruit and the other looks on without eating. This could be interpreted as the body-soul nexus; the body relishes in the samsara – the world of sensations – and the soul looks on as witness – as *karma sakshi.* In our context this is the witness and the wheel. The calmness and composure of the bird signifies that *calm of mind all passion spent*! In *Hamlet* (Act V Scene 2) Shakespeare has written:

There's a divinity that shapes our ends,
Rough-hew them how we will –

Even when we err and commit mistakes the touch of the divine rectifies our actions; but what is required is our preparedness. This brings us to *Transformation:*

My breath runs in a subtle rhythmic stream;
It fills my members with a might divine:
I have drunk the Infinite like a giant's wine.
Time is my drama or my pageant dream.
Now are my illumined cells joy's flaming scheme

And changed my thrilled and branching nerves to fine
Channels of rapture opal and hyaline
For the influx of the Unknown and the Supreme.

I am no more a vassal of flesh,
A slave to Nature and her leaden rule;
I am caught no more in the senses' narrow mesh.
My soul unhorizoned widens to measureless sight,
My body is God's happy living tool,
My spirit a vast sun of deathless light.

There is a deep recognition in this transformed stage of the existence of the self and the body in a temporal mould as well. Life breath still pulses through the veins composed of flesh and blood. And *Time is my drama or my pageant dream!* As the contexts of this sonnet has been widely discussed there is little point in overstating its vision. The idea it conveys is caught in the last three lines succinctly:

My soul unhorizoned widens to measureless sight,
My body is God's happy living tool,
My spirit a vast sun of deathless light.

Soul, body, and spirit are infused with a spiritual transformation. What is interesting is that while the transformed status of both the soul and the spirit are described in terms of the negative: *unhorizoned,* and *deathless, the* body has attained the transformed status of being God's happy living tool! This feeling of oceanic oneness with the divine is a poetic feeling of being on fire! The Tamil poet Subramanya Bharathi sang in a very short poem; *when I thrust my finger into the fire, O Nandalala, I feel the exultation of your touch!*

As Rumi also says: I used to be raw/Then I was cooked/Now... on fire.

In the domain of our ignorance where we live our everyday lives the touch of the divine is easily overlooked. The soul, or that aesthetic being in human beings, constantly reminds us of our divine origin and the process of Godward becoming. In his *Dream Boat*, Sri Aurobindo states this so clearly:

Who was it that came to me in a boat made of dream-fire,
With his flame brow and his sun-gold body?
Melted was the silence into a sweet secret murmur,
"Do you come now? Is the heart's fire ready?"

Hidden in the recesses of the heart something shuddered,
It recalled all that the life's joy cherished,
Imaged the felicity it must leave lost forever,
And the boat passed and the gold god vanished.

Now within the hollowness of the world's breast inhabits –
For the love died and the old joy ended –
Void of a felicity that has fled, gone forever,
And the gold god and the dream boat come not.

The psychic opening and aspiration are not easily come by. The touch of the divine passes us by in all our mundanity and because we simply love being in the grip of ignorance cherishing its imaged felicity! In the case of Sri Aurobindo the transformation is achieved through a consistent pursuit of the divine through the triple levels of body, life and mind. His is a life of yoga. But as he himself has noted – *all life is yoga!*

Now this is how he phrases it in his Life Divine:

> The liberation of the will follows upon the liberation in knowledge and is its dynamic consequence; it is knowledge that purifies, it is truth that liberates: evil is the fruit of a spiritual ignorance and it will disappear only by the growth of a spiritual consciousness and the light of spiritual knowledge. The division of our being from the being of others can only be healed by removing the divorce of our nature from the inner soul-reality, by abolishing the veil between our becoming and our self-being, by bridging the remoteness of our individuality in Nature from the Divine Being who is the omnipresent Reality in Nature and above Nature.
>
> But the last division to be removed is the scission between this Nature and the Supernature which is the Self-Power of the Divine Existence. (631-32)

It may not be difficult even for a general reader to recognise how the intellect images the experience in a philosophical mode and how the similar experience is explored in a poetic mode. Perhaps Sri Aurobindo himself would have felt an immediacy and natural affinity toward the poetic because he was essentially a poet. In the poetic world all binaries are resolved and evened out. The experience of integral yoga manifests itself effortlessly through the rhythmic tongue of poetry. The key concepts in context of course are *being* and *becoming*. In poetic terms there is an inner transformation that occurs when the touch of the divine is internalised and realised. This is a process of inner becoming a definite state-change. But in spiritual terms this is the touch of the essential being, tracing a being calm of mind and all passion spent! In our ceaseless exploration of reality we trace the arc of inward and Godward becoming, and once the ascent and descent are integrated what is left is the abiding spirit, neither *I* nor *Thou*.

Now, one of the major reasons as to why Sri Aurobindo is not an easy poet to grasp and to digest – a point that I mentioned earlier – is his disproportionate image (churned out by the discourses that arose around his life, his work and the several Ashrams, a point I have discussed in greater detail elsewhere in this book) as a great intellectual, a true mystic, and an even greater Rishi. Granted, his works are ponderous and huge, his range of intellectual preoccupation extremely large, his methodology of explication quite complicated, and his scholarship immense. His works overshadow him without doubt. From political pamphlets to philosophical treatises, from translation of key Vedic and Upanishadic texts to commentaries on the Gita, from Yoga through Metaphysics to poetry and linguistic theorising, his writings are definitely prolific and his thought process suitably complex. Sri Aurobindo, the *Renaissance Man,* desired and hungered at every stage to reflect deeply on life issues and articulate its intricate interior and arterial nuances. However, it is most certainly in his poetic compositions that we sense and perceive his inner turmoil a little more comprehensively. And this fact is borne out by his sheer dedication to the form. As is so very well known, he resorted to poetry as a means of spiritual ascension (Read his letters on *Savitri.)*

Now at this point there could be several raised eye brows: should not one limit his spiritual ascendency as revealed in his epic *Savitri* as truly authentic, and leave the other poems as belonging to another order and structure? However, it necessarily follows in my contention that Sri Aurobindo is essentially a poet and it is largely through his poetic narratives that we can get various glimpses of his inner struggles toward godhead. And more so in his short, easily accessible pieces, where length does not hamper nor form constrain. Here also as with everything else the range is certainly vast. But he returned to poetry at every point in his life and never ceased to experiment with verse, vision, form and structure. The poems may not constitute a linear narrative explicating his vision – and that was never his idea – but we can piece them together as a parts of a large jigsaw puzzle on our way to get the bigger picture. In the three part division of our experience of Godward becoming as we have seen poetry does appear as an appropriate tool of explication.

Like everyone else Sri Aurobindo lived in an earthly mould but quite unlike many others he lived an interior life where spiritual truths were a little more real and tangible than the usual everyday objects that we are wont to live with. He writes:

> Now within the hollowness of the world's breast inhabits –
> For the love died and the old joy ended –
> Void of a felicity that has fled, gone forever,
> And the gold god and the dream boat come not.

The anguish here is an anguish of the gods, a supra-human despair, a profound remorse at having missed the boat and the boatman, and the agonising thought that the boat may not return forever! What is left is the sheer hollowness of the world! This could be just an evanescent crises in an otherwise fulfilling life of a self-realised yogi, but nevertheless his spiritual tenacity and unwavering commitment to those higher values would make the agony even more intense.

Hard-core Aurobindonians might find this angle of pursuit a little shaky: for them Sri Aurobindo had left a clear trail of the spiritual quest, one that reveals a steady ascent and how could one even speak of struggle or despair?

But in the life of a true poet struggle and calamity are everyday affairs; they are milestones *en route* to the higher realisation.

Adi Sankara, the *paramahamsa* of Advaita, a profoundly intellectual philosopher, in his all too brief but intense life has had several such moments of spiritual crisis. In a marvellously moving poem attributed to him titled *Sivaparadhaksamapana stotram* he writes:

> *Ayur nasyati pasyatam pratidinam yati ksayam yauvanam*
> *Pratyayanti gatah punarna divasa kalo jagatbhakshakah*
> *Lakshmistoyatarangabhangachapala vidychalam jivitam*
> *Tasmanam saranagatam saranada tvam raksha rakshadhuna*

Life ebbs away each second each minute, Kala – time – is the eater of the world, and Lakshmi, the Goddess of Wealth is as transient and fickle as the breaking of the wave of water; *jivitam* – life – is as evanescent as lightning – *vidyuchalam-* and each moment life ebbs away. Youth, like all these is equally transient and disappears in no time at all. Therefore I seek refuge in Thee, O Lord Siva, I am the *Saranagata,* the refugee. Spiritual suffering and existential anguish lead the seeker toward the path of bhakthi, *sarana.* It is noteworthy that Sri Aurobindo highlights bhakthi as forming the essential narrative spirit of the Bhagavad Gita.

In ultimate surrender the self and soul come together and the spirit manifests itself transforming subject and experience. As the Irish poet, W B Yeats would phrase it: *who can then distinguish the dancer from the dance?* In this dimension of interior transformation anything can be achieved. To believe Sri Aurobindo, *that is one reason why a spiritual call must be accepted as imperative and take precedence over all other claims, intellectual, ethical, social, that belong to the domain of the Ignorance. (The Life Divine, 630)*

To the aspiring soul there are three levels: ascent, descent, and integration. The poem titled *Ascent* speaks about the experience of the self, soul and spirit, escaping from the clutches of raw nature to drown in the bliss of godhead, the *Swan of the supreme and spaceless ether…*

> Spirit, pass out of thyself; Soul, escape from the clutch of Nature.
> All thou hast seen cast from thee, O Witness.
> Turn to the Alone and the Absolute, turn to the Eternal:
> Be only eternity, peace and silence,
> O world-transcending nameless Oneness,
> Spirit immortal.

The second movement of this poem is a passage *Beyond the Silence.*

> Soul, exceed life's boundaries; Spirit, surpass the universe.
> Outclimbing the summits of Nature,
> Transcending and uplifting the soul of the finite,
> Rise with the world in thy bosom,
> O Word gathered into the heart of the Ineffable.
> One with the Eternal, live in his infinity,
> Drowned in the Absolute, found in the Godhead,
> wandering winged through the universe,
> Spirit immortal.

The Spirit descends as grace and effects the third and completing process of transformation. Mystical poetry of this quality of course transcends the borderlands of the binary and spiritual integration is realised. This is the true potential of all mankind as Sri Aurobindo would phrase it. Such is his optimism and faith in the humankind's transformation, that Sri Aurobindo devised a whole system of yoga – integral Yoga – to aid in the ascent and integration. In *Descent* we read:

> All the world is changed to a single oneness;
> Souls undying, infinite forces, meeting,
> Join in God-dance weaving a seamless Nature,
> Rhythm of the Deathless.

This is the outcome of the experience of *satchitananda* – the beatitude of the Spiritual transformation. For those of us who are deeply concerned with the fate of mankind and nature at large, this vision of inward becoming and transcendental being would strike certain noble chords. This amazing yogi-poet and intellectual in his unceasing struggle for transcending being and becoming, never ceases to excite or amaze. And that assures his continued relevance in our midst.

Notes

1. Adi Sankara's verse cited from the translation by Swami Chinamayananda. *Forgive Me: Sivaparadhakshamapana stotram (Adi Sankara)* Bombay: Central Chinmaya Mission Trust, 1982.
2. All extracts from Sri Aurobindo are from *The Life Divine*, first published in *Arya,* August 1914- January 1919, 5th Edition and 7th impression with author's corrections, published by the Sri Aurobindo Ashram, 1982.
3. Poetry extracts are from *Collected Poems,* 1st edition 4th impression, published by the Sri Aurobindo Ashram, 1986.

CHAPTER 3

Prakriti and the Manifestations of Spiritual Consciousness: Dimensions of Nature and the Vedic Lineage of an Eco-Discourse in Sri Aurobindo's *Savitri*[1]

Her being's fibre reached out vibrating
And claimed deep union with its outer selves,
And on the heart's chords made pure to seize all tones
Heaven's subtleties of touch unwearing forced
More vivid raptures than earth's life can bear.
[Savitri, Book Eleven, Canto One, Lines 155-58.]

I sacrifice not earth to happier worlds.
[Savitri, Book Eleven, Canto One, Line 767]

All happily grows towards knowledge and towards bliss…
An inner law of beauty shapes our lives…
[Savitri, Book Seven, Canto Five, Lines309;316]

Humans learn what to value and how to care for it through their cultural traditions and upbringing. The absence of a cultural basis for valuing the land we inhabit is the root of human behaviour that degrades and pollutes our world. Devaluing, destroying, and removing cultures which have discerned and received other ways of learning and valuing the earth intensifies the downward spiral of degrading our landscapes. Devaluing people and their ways of living destroys diversity in thought, habit, community, and ecosystems.

Robbin Morris Collin, in The Apocalyptic Vision,
Environmentalism and a Wider Embrace
(ISLE 13.1.Winter 2006; 1-11)

By way of an Introduction

Any inquisitive reader of this essay, unless otherwise he/he is familiar with what goes under the name of ecocriticism as a critical theory and practice, is bound to pause and inquire as to what could be the relevance of, and connection between, the concepts mentioned in the title *Eco-discourse and Sri Aurobindo's Savitri.* There are many points here that need to be clarified beforehand. Those readers who are familiar with ecocriticism would immediately conclude that this essay is conceived along the conceptual lines of ecologically sensitive theories that are rampant in academic circles in India these days, and strives to establish connections between the text mentioned and nature or the natural. While on the other and, studies on the work of Sri Aurobindo are fairly innumerable and his poetry and poetics have been close examined by several insightful critics, there is little space for anything new to come up or be drawn up. And *Savitri* has been read and explained at great length by innumerable critics and scholars. Obviously, there is hardly anything left for the latter-day critic to explicate or describe at length, for it is usual for Aurobindonians to fall back upon the work of the master for explicating his own texts. Thus there is bound to be some curiosity among the genuinely interested scholars and students of Sri Aurobindo. What follows is an attempt to approach the work of the yogi from an entirely new point of view. I have resorted to sources other than the ones usually relied upon by renowned Aurobindo scholars. Without being prescriptive, let me claim that such different approach or approaches would yield surprising results. That is probably what the master himself would have desired, for he was in fact a *practical dreamer*. He implicated his own self in his philosophical texts and strongly *believed* in his ideals and ideas. As I have said elsewhere, he moved among his ideas as we would move among tables and chairs; they were too real for him. If transformation of the human's being was his desire he tuned his own life toward that end. As the scholars have pointed out if the *Life Divine* was the philosophical exploration of his ideals, *Savitri* was its poetic realisation.

In this essay, I have resorted to the arguments and observations of many academics and critics who have pursued the intrinsic relationship between nature and human nature. After a brief intervention into the ecocritical and eco-aesthetic theorising, I move on to a reading of *Savitri.* If the conventional scholars of Sri Aurobindo find themselves a little unsettled by my unorthodox approach, I would appeal to that part of their Indian mind that would have cultivated the argumentative tradition that Amartya Sen has justified in his work of that name. After all, it is important to keep one's own critical mind and inquisitive brain clearly focused when approaching the work of a supreme intellectual like Sri Aurobindo.

The Terrain: The Holistic Nature of Spiritual Aesthetic

In the contexts of discussing the interface between nature and human nature it is my contention that one needs to move beyond any kind of limiting categories in terms of culture, outlook, geography and history, either of any western or its *other* – eastern – kinds, and adopt a holistic view. Of course, I fully recognise the inordinate nature of this claim, *fundamentally* because primarily, any claims to a spiritualised awareness (in terms of the sacred and the holy) is generally regarded solely as the prerogative of humans, and the non-human world is of course deprived of any such possibilities, and, further, the discourse of spirituality itself is often marginalised as inapplicable in the *practical world* of everyday affairs and the life of the senses. Moreover when I argue for the inclusive vision inspired by the visionary culture of a non-western world[2], I also recognise that the discriminative and theoretically oriented reader would by nature tend to read my essay as prefabricated in a postcolonial mode and *read* it within a *given grid.* Given the nature of these situations, I would, at the very outset, implore that what follows be read as attempting to formulate a continuity in the ecocritical debate, and contextualise my arguments within the framework of the intellectual inquiry that seeks to theorise the human nature interface. Literature and ideas of nature within and without the aesthetic debate, I hold, are never homogenous, but on the other hand marked by human difference, geography, culture, location, gender, class, race, and the psyche. Nevertheless there does occur an interface, a territory commonly shared, cutting across all boundaries and differences, where in the experience of the spiritual occurs; and this is an area that falls beyond history and ideology. I fully understand that it is never the same for all at all times, however, the experience of the spiritual is unique and dissimilar at the same time! It is my contention that my essay shapes itself within such a region or a *non-region.* My arguments are couched in the logic of the senses and the rationality of discourse, but by the very virtue of my terrain, they are dislocated from any west-east discrimination. The spiritual is a-historic, but experiential and at the same time proffers enough space for dialogical engagement as mystics of all times have realised.

Ecosystem Culture and Biosphere Culture

In his *Literature of Nature: An International Source Book*[3], Patrick D. Murphy draws attention to the two major types of stories that people have usually told about the *spaces* they inhabit and the *places* they live. In more ways than one, these stories could be seen to "delineate the difference between a planetary orientation and a global outlook, or what Gary Snyder has referred to as ecosystem culture and biosphere culture…. The ecosystem culture is attentive to local particularity and the benefits of heterogeneity, while the biosphere culture relentlessly attempts to homogenise the peoples of the world in the interests of transnational economics." Murphy warns the sensitive *ecocritic* to be vigilant and to be wary of falling into prescriptive critical formulations, and suggests the three-fold sense of place, which he demarcates as *geographic location, historical location, and geo-psychic or self-aware location.* (Murphy, 1998:xiv) Such a clear-cut understanding, I believe, is necessary in our approach to non-western discourses of nature and human nature.

Ecological Criticism as it is practiced in our academies is certainly Anglo-American in its inception and outlook, but however, it has opened up multiple points of entry and debate over the human and non-human nexus or divide. Both the local and the global discourses have gone in to its making.

Ecocriticism and Intrinsic Value[4]

In a land like India with its heterogeneous culture and checkered history, the narratives linking place and humans are innumerable, couched in diverse perceptions and points of view, and filtered through multiple discourses over a long period of time. Geographically, historically and geo-psychically Indian narratives afford pluralistic and complex readings. Philosophy, religion and poetry have a deep history in this part of the world, as much as oppression, domination, and ideologies of resistance and subversions.[5]

In more ways than one the emergence of ecocriticism in the academic world has signaled a resuscitation of the *idea of intrinsic value in nature* that has almost come to be buried under the rubble of a postindustrial culture that constantly seeks to obliterate all differences into making the omnivorous discourse of globalisation and technocracy as monolithic and one-dimensional. Perhaps this return to nature could even be mocked as mere retrogression toward the European Romantic tradition of linking the human and the non-human into some sort of metaphysical essence. Or ecologically sensitive critical theorising could also be demonised as a debilitating attempt to reinstate the grand narratives of a misplaced cultural humanism, in the lines of high modernist elitism. A third probability is that of a universally developing urban culture demonising its own predatory roles in the haloed light of a forfeited primitive human culture! Either way the very suggestion of the notion of sacred or spiritual at the heart of nature's being is sure to invite many raised brows in our present day world. Nevertheless the direction that ecologically sensitive critical theory is currently pursuing seeking to reinforce idea and action in the material plane (a union of the spirit and matter in different scale), in terms of environmental justice, is a sure sign of not having lost its way *in the dreary sands of dead habit…*

The story of human nature relationship is the story of the fall from grace, from a life sharing the sacred to one of utilizing mere resource. The absence of a cultural basis for valuing the land we inhabit is perhaps the root of human behaviour that degrades and pollutes our world! The values that ancient Indian tradition (diverse, multidimensional, manifold, heterogeneous and different) invokes are spiritual and a-temporal. They are rooted in a sense of place and time of course, but transcendental in their significance. They could be seen as proffering both a *bioregional and ecosystem* view of life and living. The elemental symbolism of the Vedic and Upanishadic mantras are rooted in a culture of place and value while the ritualistic and sacred qualities that they evoke are trans-human and trans-natural. Above all the ancient Indian cultural outlook was a constant recognition of the sacred at the heart of all being. This notion of the *sacred* does not devalue the phenomenal world of the senses but on the other hand endows it with deeper significance and value. Ecology might be the socially evoked unified and holisitic view of nature for the present, but the ecological vision that a poetic insight engendered through the spiritual, would nevertheless enhance all qualities of life and living, both in terms of the human and non-human, for its significance is not historically conditioned[6].

Indian thought is more concerned with seeking connections than separateness. Even from the very beginnings the conceptual concerns of the ancient Indian reveals a leaning toward the holistic and a seeking after the interconnectedness of all and everything. *Ekam sad vipra bahudha vadanti*, says the Rig Veda (1.164.46), the Existent is one, but the sages express it variously. There exists a spatio-temporal interrelatedness of all existence in a continuum of quality and this is further embedded in the notion of all life in the world as forming one whole continuous interrelated being – *vasudaiva kudumbakam*. The earth and all its life forms – living and non-living alike are held to be of equal value. [This is not tantamount by extension to stating that the Indian values of quality and being are universal values, like the widely held view in the present day world of market capitalism that economic prosperity ensures moral superiority!] Nevertheless, in a land like India with its heterogeneous culture and checkered history, the narratives linking place and humans are innumerable, couched in diverse perceptions and points of view, and filtered through multiple discourses over a long period of time. Geographically, historically, and geo-psychically Indian narratives afford pluralistic and complex readings. Philosophy, religion, and poetry have a deep history in this part of the world, as much as oppression, domination, and ideologies of resistance and subversions.

A great deal of western understanding of India revolves round the religion of the Hindus which is generally spiritual and theistic. However, we need to remember that to speak of an Indian spiritual tradition is not to deny the continued existence and significance of materialist discourses alongside. In *The Argumentative Indian*[7], renowned Economist Amartya Sen has noted:

> An adequately inclusive understanding of Indian heterodoxy is particularly important for appreciating the reach and range of heterodoxy in the country's intellectual background and diverse history. This is especially critical because of the relative neglect of the rationalist parts of Indian heritage in the contemporary accounts of India's past, in favour of concentrating on India's impressive religiosity.

Recognising the significance of this warning, we could state that a tolerance of diversity, difference and pluralism has been a distinctive characteristic of the Indian mind. Indeed this long lasting history of heterodoxy stems from the most intense and inquisitive poetic renderings of the Vedic texts, dating back to the middle of the second millennium BCE. The Vedic Vision was a poetic one, and it proffers a distinct philosophy of transformation of the human's being. In many ways the *concern of Vedic poetry is practical, namely the actual realisation in one's own person, of what it means to be fully human.* The Vedas speak of nature and human nature as intimately linked, and the destiny of human's being and that of physical nature is definitely interconnected.

Nature in the Vedas and Upanishads

The Vedas[8] are held in great reverence as the repository of sacred and revealed knowledge. The word Veda means knowledge, it is derived from the root word *vid, to know.* And knowledge for the ancient Indian was the knowledge of how to live, what to live for, and also live life in a progressively most meaningful manner, all directed towards a spiritually meaningful existence. The accent was more on being and becoming rather than doing and having. The latter were of course dependent on and concomitant with the former, drawing sustenance, directive and significance from the four fold vision of life – Dharma (the righteous path/order), Artha (meaning/material possession), Kama (love/desire) and Moksha (liberation/release). The Vedas set forth the mantra, the vision, the utterance and the directives for ritualistic existence – depending on how they were approached and read they guided the living. As with all early people's narratives the Vedas too provide two-fold significance – the exoteric or the outer and the esoteric or the inner, secretive. This is the region where the idea of being as quality occurs.

Nature in Sanskrit is *prakrti:* which could be interpreted in two ways – as the outer nature comprising all non-human being, inclusive of the physical human's being, and also the inner nature, or the essential characteristic of something. And outside nature was of course a continuation of the inner, because all being cosmic and atomic was essentially one: *aham brahmasmi*, says the Upanishad (I am Brahman, the all-pervading). We should note however, that in this ecstatic statement of enlightenment the *I* or *aham* does not refer to the individuality or outer nature, but to the essence of the soul that is ever identical with the spiritual at the heart of all being. T*at tvam asi*: that thou art. This spiritualised vision of nature and being afforded a spiritual aesthetic, because only as an aesthetic relish could the world be finally resolved. The phenomenal world (*virat*) was seen as constantly changing in a flux – it was *vivarta*, or illusion (maya) and the illumined mind can reintegrate itself in the ultimate relish or *parama ananda*, in the *dance of Siva.*

The story of human nature relationship is the story of the fall from grace, from a life sharing the sacred to one of utilising mere resource. The absence of a cultural basis for valuing the land we inhabit is the root of human behaviour that degrades and pollutes our world! The values that ancient Indian tradition (diverse, multidimensional, manifold, heterogeneous and different) invokes are spiritual and a-temporal. They are rooted in a sense of place and time of course, but transcendental in their significance. They could be seen as proffering both a *bioregional* and *ecosystem* view of life and living. The elemental symbolism of the Vedic and Upanishadic mantras are rooted in a culture of place and value while the ritualistic and sacred qualities that they evoke are trans-human and trans-natural. Above all the ancient Indian cultural outlook was a constant recognition of the sacred at the heart of all being. This notion of the sacred does not devalue the phenomenal world of the senses but on the other hand endows it with deeper significance and value. Ecology might be the socially evoked unified and holisitic view of nature for the present, but the ecological vision that a poetic insight engendered through the spiritual, would nevertheless enhance all qualities of life and living, both in terms of the human and non-human, for its significance is not historically conditioned.

Towards an Aesthetic of Nature

The Vedic vision was essentially a poetic one. The manner in which the ancient Indian approached nature and life itself was in complete recognition of a holistic and integral poetic vision. Life was seen as a process toward a progressive accumulation of wisdom. M Vannucci[9] in her study of human ecology in the Vedic hymns has argued that *knowledge* in the Vedic sense has much in common with what we call *science* and hence *truth* in the sense in which the ancient Indian seers used it was *scientific* and verifiable through the senses.

> The resis of the Veda were historical men and at least one woman, Lopamudra, even if modern critical historical analysis considers "proofs" to be insufficient. The seers/poets/scientists who formulated the hymns lived with nature that they studied and used. A strong feeling of man's participation in the universal order pervades the Veda; man is inseparable from his cosmic environment, he is not distinct from it but imbued in it (Vannucci, 1999; 62)

The Vedas according to her are a "treasure mine of information about the science of ancient man…of the way that man thought… and transmitted his knowledge to others" (37). These the seers achieved through their use of elemental symbolism.

To believe Sri Aurobindo[10], mystic poet and modern day seer:

> At one time poetry was a revelation to the race of the life of the gods and man and the meaning of the world and the beauty and power of existence, and through its vision and joy and the height and clarity of its purpose it became creative of the life of the people.... That sublime poetry with its revelation of godhead and the joy and power of life and truth and immortality or its revelation of the secrets of the self and the powers of its manifestation in man and the universe and of man's return to self-knowledge got into the very blood and mind and life of the race and made itself the fountain head of all that incessant urge to spirituality which has been its distinguishing gift and cultural motive.[11] (Sri Aurobindo, 1985; 234-35)

The Vedas are held in great reverence as the repository of sacred and revealed knowledge. The word Veda means knowledge, it is derived from the root word *vid, to know.* And knowledge for the ancient Indian was the knowledge of how to live, what to live for, and also live life in a progressively most meaningful manner, all directed towards a spiritually meaningful existence. The accent was more on being and becoming rather than doing and having. The latter were of course dependent on and concomitant with the former, drawing sustenance, directive and significance from the four fold vision of life – Dharma, Artha, Kama and Moksha. The Vedas set forth the mantra, the vision, the utterance and the directives for ritualistic existence – depending on how they were approached and read they guided the living. As with all early people's narratives the Vedas[12] too provide two fold significance – the exoteric or the outer and the esoteric or the inner, secretive.

In many ways an environmentally self-aware way and vision of life represented in the Vedic mantras and later conceptually formulated in the Upanishadic verses of a spiritual aesthetic, could be seen to antedate the historically conditioned religious doctrines and their attendant practices of a later age. The Vedic and Upanishadic aesthetics calls for a distinct understanding of a poetic vision of human and non-human life, one that could be resolved only aesthetically. Eventually, however, as Hindu system of beliefs evolved, a four-fold categorisation of life came to be formulated in terms of Dharma (the righteous path/order), Artha (meaning/ material possession), Kama (love, desire), and Moksha (liberation or release). (At every stage of life, nature played a significant role and an *aesthetic of the spiritual* would lead towards a holistic revelation of poetics – nature as metaphor and meaning, that would form the *other self of nature.*)

Ekam sad vipra bahudha vadanti, says the Rig Veda (1.164.46) the Existent is one, the sages express it variously. The Vedas are replete with elemental symbolism. Agni (fire) Vayu (air) Prthvi (earth) Akasa (ether) Ap (water) all have their gods and goddesses, Then there is Dyava-Prthvi Heaven and earth – the primeval couple. In not a single hymn of the RigVeda is heaven mentioned alone. Celebrating this togetherness of Earth and Heaven, the Vedic poet sings:

> Which of these two came earlier, which came later
> How did they come to birth? Who, O seers can discern it?
> They contain within them all that has a name
> While days and nights revolve as on a wheel.
> (quoted in Shah, 2006; 14)

In the "*Hymn of Earth*" in the Atharva Veda (the longest one containing 63 stanzas) we read:

> Whatever I dig of you, O Earth,
> May you of that have a quick replenishment
> O purifying One, may my thrust never
> Reach right into your vital points, your heart!
> (Shah, 2006; 14)

In the Vedic mantras, *Aranyani* is hailed with praises by the wind and the grasshopper, while the unbounded expanse of nature is symbolised by *Aditi.* Sacrifice symbolises the process of creative transformation in nature, and *Rta* is the fundamental Vedic concept that incorporates the cycle of seasons and rain. Varivas means openness – to create an open space or clearing, to break through the cribbed and confined space of mortal life. The desire for this openness and for release from constriction, the creation of liberating space is conveyed by the word, Varivasya (See Shah (16))

> Intelligence, give me
> The exact name of things
> Let my word be the thing itself
> Newly created by my soul
> Through me may all those
> Who have forgotten things reach them
> Through me may all those
> Who even love things may reach them.
> Juan Ramon Jimenez (quoted Shah, 2006; 23)

Thus the text of the Vedas in general and of the Rig Veda in particular discloses to us a world, which in the words of J L Mehta, philosopher, is "the unifying play of the fourfold of earth and heaven, gods and mortals, in which man dwells on earth as his home, under the heavens, in friendly commerce with the gods, with his fellow men, with things, building and making untiringly with thoughts and words and things." (Philosophy and Religion, p.278; quoted in Shah, 2006; 15-16)

> The concern of Vedic poetry is practical, namely the actual realisation in one's own person, of what it means to be fully human (Shah, 2006; 16)

The Vedic imagery is symbolic. It speaks of light and darkness and the human journey through mysterious darkness to light. But nevertheless the ancient Indians also have seen the darkness at the heart of light: *hiranmayena patrena satyasyapihitam mukham, tat tvam pusan apavrunu satyadharmaya drisyate. (The face of truth is covered by a golden disc; unveil it o Sun, that I who love theruth may behold it)*

The Upanishads, which follow the Vedas in many aspects, are on the other hand, cryptic, intellectual utterances in a much more evolved poetic mode. In the words of Sri Aurobindo,

> The Upanishads are not a revolutionary departure from the Vedic mind and its temperament and fundamental ideas, but a continuation and development and to a certain extent an enlarging transformation in the sense of bringing out into open expression all that was held covered in the symbolic Vedic speech as a mystery and a secret. It begins by taking up the imagery and the ritual symbols of the Veda and the Brahmanas and turning them in such a way as to bring out an inner and a mystic sense which will serve as a sort of psychical starting-point for its own more highly evolved and more purely spiritual philosophy.[13]

Sri Aurobindo's *Savitri*[14], as I propose to argue, is in the direct line of Vedic and Upanishadic thought, and *Nature* is used as metaphor for a state of being (in the Aurobindian scheme of things) and it reveals the hidden possibility of transformation from the material – the *inconscient* – to the spiritual – the *superconscient. Savitri* is the symbolic dawn that revels in its own secret/sacred self. The entire epic is an unfolding of the hidden possibilities of this *other self of nature.*

As pointed out earlier, Indian narratives linking place and humans are diverse and heterogeneous, couched in diverse perceptions and points of view, and filtered through multiple discourses over a long period of time. *Savitri*'s trajectory definitely reveals this close affinity to the eco-spiritual discourse, of difference and oneness, of intrinsic value in nature and the hidden possibilities of its transformation.

Sri Aurobindo's Savitri: *A Legend and a Symbol*

> *Yat sanoh sanumaruhat bhuri aspsta kartvam* (As he climbed from peak to peak he espied evermore what was to be done) cited by Sri Aurobindo in *The Secret of the Veda.*

Savitri is perhaps the nearest to a complete expression of an *aesthetic of the spiritual* that would self-reflexively lead towards a holistic revelation of experiential poetics – nature as metaphor and meaning that would form the *other self of nature*. The action in this epic poem takes place in geo-psychic realms that in Sri Aurobindo's specific terminology would be the *Overmental* regions. The poet's Yogic practices and spiritual training afforded him profound experiences in the interior spaces of the soul (which according to him constituted *the aesthetic being in man*). Savitri, is perhaps the longest poem in the English language running into *twelve Books and forty nine cantos*, and the poet consistently worked on it for nearly four decades. Taking off from a small anecdote in the *Mahabharata*, this poem is conceived as a legend and a symbol – the entire text is an unfolding of the image of aesthetic transformation in symbolic terms. My reading of select cantos and situations in this long epic would focus on how nature and human nature undergo a transforming divinisation that does not forego difference and identity.

Sri Aurobindo's vision is essentially a poetic one (very much in line with the Vedic seers), and he was always concerned with the poetic experience, both the creative and the critical aspects. His writings range from political pamphlets to sociological treatises, exegesis on the Veda, the Upanishads, and the Gita, to systematic treatises on Yoga and its various dimensions, from critical thinking on the foundations of Indian culture and history to philosophical writings on the meaning of spiritual being and the poetics of spiritual transformation. What remain common throughout his writings are this aspect of spiritual transformation and an aesthetic of spirituality. This reaches its culmination in his two major contributions: in T*he Life Divine* this is achieved through sound philosophical ratiocination, and in *Savitri* as an aesthetic experience.

Based on his own intense personal yogic experience and on clear-sighted, poetic and interpretative exegesis of the Vedic mantras, Sri Aurobindo avows that *all life is Yoga.* What he intends here is a possibility to willfully integrate the human will with its divine counterpart – the integration of the inner and outer nature – a union, that would spiritualise all being ultimately. All existence, in his vision, is a pervading of the Spirit. This is not mere pantheism – for the concept of God that Sri Aurobindo resorts to is not one that is monolithic nor homogenous. (cf *Iswara* as personal godhead) the entire cosmic play or Lila of the Divine is the transformation of life from its merely material, *inconscient* state (in Aurobindian terminology) to that of being gradually and systematically self-conscious and spiritually *superconscient.*

As Sri Aurobindo argued, from Matter to Life and to Mind there is a progressive evolution of the already *involuted* spirit; and now that such an evolution from Matter to Mind had been achieved there is further possibility of attaining the other steps in the future evolution[15]. Sri Aurobindo on the strength of his spiritual achievement categorises those as: *Higher mind, Illumined mind, Intuition,* and *Overmind* – stages to be reached before achieving the complete divinisation of all being (matter inclusive), the Supramental being. In *Savitri* he finds the right situation for developing his scheme of spiritual evolution. One needs to keep in mind that the poetics of Savitri is in direct line with the Vedic, and the symbolism is deliberately *elemental.* Sri Aurobindo's involvement with the Vedic texts and the mantras in Sanskrit language afforded him an entry into the profound elemental quality of the language of poetry. *Savitri* is created as *dhyanamantra.* And the desired attitude of reading is also to be meditative. A few instances from the long poem would explicate this:

> In the enormous spaces of the self
> The body now seemed only a wandering shell
>
> (Book I, canto v, 291-92)

In the *Overmental aesthetic* as evinced by Sri Aurobindo, the highest intensity of poetic speech and poetic vision combine to give rise to *mantra.*

> As blooms a flower in an unvisited place
> The wide world knew not yet the inhabitant flame,
> Yet something deeply stirred and dimly knew;
> There was a movement and a passionate call,
> A rainbow dream, a hope of golden change;
> Some secret wing of expectation beat,
> A growing sense of something new and rare
> And beautiful stole across the heart of time.
>
> (Book IV, Canto ii, 289-96)

The *mantra* or the highest intensity of poetic expression is reached when sound and sense (*sabda* and *artha*) combine in the right order, as it happens in the following instance where the nuances of the language are captured:

Only sometimes small thoughts rose and fell
Like quiet waves upon a silent sea
Or ripples passing over a lonely pool
When a stray stone disturbs its dreaming rest.
(Book VII, Canto vi, 405-408)

The text of *Savitri* is replete with unique instances like these, however, it is when the poet moves into the terrain where the geography of the imagination intercepts the ordered measures of poetic utterance that he excels himself and appears to touch the highest possibilities of expression. Here in this instance the poet depicts the slow movement of the trio – Satyavan, Death and Savitri – into the realms of the beyond:

Luminous he moved away; behind him Death
Went slowly with his noiseless tread, as seen
In dream-built fields a shadowy herdsman glides
Behind some wanderer from his voiceless herds,
And Savitri moved behind eternal Death,
Her mortal pace was equaled with the god's.
Wordless she traveled in her lover's steps,
Planting her human feet where his had trod,
Into the perilous silences beyond.
(Book IX, Canto I, 211-219)

To read *Savitri* is to witness a tremendous adventure in the interior realms; to witness and participate in a multidimensional quest. Because *Savitri* is cast in the mould of great poetry – Mahakavya – the requisite state of mind is one of openness and humility similar to that of prayer, for each word and each phrase should ring in a "solitude and an immensity," heard in the "listening spaces of the soul," in the "inner acoustic space," and seized by the deeper self. "To embellish life with beauty," writes Sri Aurobindo in The *Future Poetry* (p.243), "is only the most outward function of art and poetry, to make life more intimately beautiful and noble and great and full of meaning is its higher office, but its highest comes when the poet becomes the seer and reveals to man his eternal self and the godheads of its manifestation." And this highest function is what he has achieved in this work. And he was convinced that:

Our souls can visit in great lonely hours
Still regions of imperishable Light (I iv 40)

The poem is replete with images of nature, the outer and the inner. And Sri Aurobindo wields the English language with expertise and ease in order to capture the multiple nuances of the spiritual experience. The Tantric dimensions of the Yogi's experience are so very unique and in an equally unique manner *Savitri* enfolds the rapture and distress, the pain and the pleasure, the effort and the ease. (See Book VII canto v, 206ff)

The poem opens with the symbol dawn, with the stark opening lines:

> It was the hour before the gods awake.

The entire time span of the poem is concentrated on the fateful day of Satyavan's death and Savitri's encounter with the dark god, because as the opening canto reminds us, *in her there was the anguish of the gods.*(199) and h*er nature felt all Nature as its own.* (275) Nature is not merely on the outside, but it connects to the soul, the psychic being in Sri Aurobindo's scheme of things: *God found in Nature, Nature fulfilled in God* (I, iii, 533). After the process of divinisation, as Sri Aurobindo visualises this, the raw nature in us is transformed – we continue to act in this world but the action is transformed spiritually. We read in the *Essays on the Gita*:

> ...action is possible without the subjection of the soul to the normal degraded functioning of the modes of Nature. That functioning depends on the mental, vital, and physical limitation into which we are cast; it is a deformation, an incapacity, a wrong or depressed value imposed on us by the mind and life in matter. When we grow into the spirit, this Dharma or inferiors law of Nature is replaced by the immortal Dharma of the Spirit; there is the experience of a free immortal action, a divine illimitable knowledge, a transcendent power, an unfathomable repose.... (We) have the thing we seek in us, but we have in practice to evolve it out of the inferior forms of our nature.[16]

Nature has a secret purpose and meaning and that is this divine fulfillment. This insight is what has inspired the poet to construct a vast multidimensional epic round a simple theme of love and death. The image of love and death is raised into a symbol for a spiritualised transformation. The entire poem is a study in human and nonhuman nature. The action takes place in the inner dimensions of being. There are two major Yogic journeys in this immense epic – that of Aswapathy's and later of Savitri's.

Sri Aurobindo has transformed a minor narrative in the *Mahabharata* into an epic of spiritual and symbolic significance. The tale of Satyavan and Savitri is simple enough. King Aswapathy has a daughter Savitri, who falls in love with Satyavan, the son of a dispossessed and blind king Dyumatsena. It is foretold that Satyavan is to die within an year of their marriage. Savitri is undaunted and they are married. When Satyavan dies at the destinied time, Savitri awaits the Lord of Death to come and possess his soul. She follows the soul into the nether realms. Despite her repeated requests Yama, the Lord of death is unrelenting in granting her the life of Satyavan. Nevertheless she persists and is finally able to overcome death with her perseverance and single-minded commitment. Satyavan is finally reunited with Savitri in an eternal life of happiness.

In the dimension of the symbol, the two kings – Aswapathy and Dyumatsena – represent power and knowledge. Knowledge needs to reflect on its own self and power requires willful insight so as to be just and non-oppressive. And Savitri herself is the embodiment of the goddess of that name – the harbinger of the great transformation. Dyumatsena – the *Lord of the Shining Hosts*, the King of Knowledge here, in the lower hemisphere, *Aparardha*[17] (as opposed to the higher *Parardha*), and father of Satyavan, falls blind and thus loses his kingdom. (At the level of symbol this is Knowledge without insight). His son Satyavan, symbolising the growing Soul of Man, a prince, a king to be, who cannot live without the support of light and truth in the darkness of this creation and therefore is destined to die within a year. Aswapathy, Savitri's father, is the Lord of the Horse (*ashva*, horse in the Vedas is a symbol of power, energy, and force in opposition to *gauh*, cow or ray of light, as a symbol of knowledge). Here in the lower hemisphere Aswapathy is involved in *Tapasya* – concentrated spiritual effort – dedicated to the Divine Mother, Savitri, "goddess of the Supreme Truth" calling her to support his spiritual work on earth with hers. In the event of her not supporting, his work has no significant future, since he has no son to continue it (very much in line with the ancient Indian thinking).

The goddess Savitri having promised Aswapathy any boon he would ask for, did not give him the progeny he wanted – many sons – because she knew that without Dyumatsena first regaining his sight and his kingdom there would be no future for it, and all the endeavours of Aswapathy would be fruitless (Knowledge without the power to transform it becomes mere tinsel). This is the reason why her human embodiment Savitri, when desired by the Lord of Death to seek any boon she wished asks for Dyumatsena's sight and his kingdom first.

This symbolic potential of the story afforded Sri Aurobindo with the format of a spiritual transformation that informs his entire philosophical system that was grounded in the Vedic order. Aswapthy undergoes several yogic experiences that transcend the phenomenal world and looks into the heart of being. The first segment of the long poem narrates his own inner journeys and explorations. He resurfaces in the real world with the assurance that the goddess Savitri the goddess of the Sun, *savita*, would herself reincarnate in earthly form and hasten the divine transformation. Savitri, on the other hand also undergoes the yogic journey, albeit of a different nature (if Aswapathy's is extensive, hers is intensive), and equips herself for the final transformation of all life. She has to undergo the entire gamut of human experience, the joy of love, the pangs of separation, the agony of death and the ordeal of foreknowledge of death and "the parable for the search of the soul". The third part of the epic is set apart for the great dialogue with Death – Savitri's rhetorical reasonings and Death's answers. (This definitely has Upanishadic overtones in terms of language, imagery and situation.)

Perhaps the entire poem is too complex and replete with symbols, and the enormity of its structure could even put off any simple minded reader. But considering the massive scheme and complicated structure it is unique in conception and execution, exploring the ceaseless miracle of the self in nature and its ultimate divinisation[18]. The poem is not meant to be merely read and *understood*, it is conceived as an exercise in meditation and inner listening with the *ear of ear* as the Veda puts it.

We read in Savitri:

> Heaven is too high for outstretched hands to seize.
> This Light comes not by struggle or by thought;
> In the mind's silence the Transcendent acts
> And the hushed heart hears the unuttered Word.
> (Book III, Canto ii, 204-07)

The great transformation or the divinisation of inconscient matter is achieved through the descent of the spirit. And the "hushed heart" needs to be prepared and listen for the "unuttered word". In the Aurobindian scheme of things, Nature is not merely matter or a term that describes the natural forms other than the human. He looks upon nature as the foundation for all life forms to generate from. It is a manifestation of the Divine Spirit that is *involuted* in it. Nevertheless it is *inconscient* and ignorant. There is a vibrant horizontal movement of the innate energy in Nature that passes through all matter, and still there is another subtle vertical dimension of this manifestation as well, that passes through and flowers forth as Life, the vital energy. Here too there is this double dimension of horizontality and verticality that coexists. Ultimately the vertical dimension of energy realises itself in the nature of Mind and the mental planes. Eventually as Sri Aurobindo visualises it, the vertical thrust would guide the evolution of the *Supermind.* Thus the transformation of nature would eventually be completed with the complete divinisation of all being. This is the objective of the *Purnayoga* (a distinct version of Yoga defined as *Integral Yoga* in Aurobindian terms) as he envisioned it, because yoga is a self-reflexive process that hastens the process of nature.

In *The Life Divine*, Sri Aurobindo's philosophical *magnum opus*, we read: "A consciousness- force, everywhere inherent in Existence, acting even when concealed, is the creator of the worlds, the occult secret of Nature."[19] This self-conscious force has a double aspect in Nature – it is Ignorance as well as Knowledge. In physical Nature the state of matter is inert, *inconscient, ignorant, and nescient.* This is the *avidly* (usually translated as ignorance, or the absence of *vidya*) state, but eventually in the evolutionary process, Consciousness gains in terms of Knowledge – *vidya* –, as it blossoms forth in Life and later Mind. This is the process of regaining of its psychic selfhood. Although this would appear to be a reading of all and everything in a generalised, universalising manner, Sri Aurobindo insists that difference and separateness too are at the heart of things. He speaks of the *essentiality*, *commonality* and *individuality* (Transcendental, Universal, and Individual) of things, "*but the three together and not one by itself are the eternal terms of existence.*" (*The Life Divine*, p 381 ff) And in the nature of all being:

> All evolution is in essence a heightening of the force of consciousness in the manifest being so that it may be raised into the greater intensity of what is still unmanifest, from matter to life, from life into mind, from the mind into the spirit. (p 726)

This evolutionary growth into the supramental state is what he visualises as the process of life divine ("divine being" and "divine living")

Thus Sri Aurobindo's aesthetics is quite integral to his spiritual system. It is characteristic of him that his poetry and thought form one coherent whole. They are expressions of his own unique spiritual experiences and realisations. For him, man's phenomenal earthly existence is "real" and he visualises with god-like intensity the topography of human evolution. The ultimate divinisation of the human being would bring about a superhuman being – not a Superman in the Nietzschean sense, but a spiritually evolved superman. The consciousness that is *involuted* in Nature has to vertically ascend through all the other grades of being only to gradually realise the Divine Gnosis. This is the ultimate purpose of all existence as Sri Aurobindo envisions it. Now Nature has a great significance in all this ascent descent and integration – it is the foundation for this divine transformation. *Savitri* is a major poetic attempt to dramatise the realisation of this other self of nature. He wrote later in a letter:

> I used *Savitri* as means of ascension. I began with it on a certain mental level, each time I could reach a higher level I rewrote it from that level. In fact *Savitri* has not been regarded by me as a poem to be written and finished, but as a field of experimentation to see how far poetry could be written from one's own yogic consciousness and how that could be made creative. (SABCL, XXVI, p.229)[20]

As in the Upanishads, which according to Sri Aurobindo, are the highest type of poetry, the aesthetic harmony in the Absolute would lead to a principle of Love. The Upanishad extols the principle of self-renunciation and abandonment – *tyaga*, and the ultimate relish that follows this process. Sri Aurobindo's experience which he has created in terms of Aswapathy's as he surrenders to the divine is hardly different:

> All nature felt again the single bliss;
> There was no cleavage between soul and soul,
> There was no barrier between world and God.
>
> The circle of the little self was gone;
> The separate being could no more be felt;
> It disappeared and knew itself no more
> Lost in the spirit's wide identity.
> His nature grew a movement of the All…
> Infinity swallowed him into shoreless trance.
> (Book III Canto iii 74 ff)

When the little self of being is revealed for what it is and unites with the larger will of the divine all distinctions and differences are seen for what they are, intrinsically meaningful and spiritually charged. The One in the many and the many in the One, is a mystical oceanic experience, and *Savitri* leads the reader directly into such a liberating aesthetic experience. In the final analysis this long epic would focus on how nature and human nature undergo a transforming divinisation that does not forego difference and identity. And this is the spiritual aesthesis that Sri Aurobindo visualised. This holistic transformation of the involuted sphere of all nature is a desire of the earth's ecological self. The charmed circle that *Savitri* weaves together is the charm of ascent, descent and integration.

The wisdom of ecological criticism as we have already seen has been to reestablish vital connections with nature. When once the living relationship has been rediscovered nature will come to be looked upon less and less as mere resource and its sacred other self would slowly come to light. In our collective globalised march of development we tend to devalue everything, because the market capitalism entertains only price and cost. Value and significance are perhaps a thing of the past and are already under the rubble of the garbage heap we keep discarding day by day. Perhaps if we were to resuscitate the collective cultural value of a lost time and of a people marginalised or even misunderstood, we could still save this, our lonely planet. All our preservation, conservation, biodiversity management and environmental justice movements would hasten us back to the time when nature could hold forth meaning and value. After all, there is this underlying aesthetic value that holds all life together and makes it collectively meaningful. And a realisation of this would mean a step towards the aesthetics of the spiritual. As Sri Aurobindo writes in *Savitri:*

> The Spirit shall take up the human play,
> This earthly life become the life divine. (710)

In my reading of *Savitri* I have attempted to reintegrate spiritual values into environmental critical debate. Such an "eco-spiritually oriented environmental stewardship can be a mechanism that strengthens respect for nature by enabling people to centre their values upon the notion that there is a cosmic ordinance and a divine law which must be maintained. … Eco-spirituality if globally manifested, can also provide the values necessary for an environmentally caring world and will not advance a blind belief in economic growth at all costs, creating in its wake greed, poverty, inequality, and injustice as well as environmental destruction."[21]

The ancient Indian view of life was a constant recognition of the sacred at the heart of all being, and as I have argued earlier, this notion of the *sacred* does not devalue the phenomenal world of the senses but a recognition of this aspect of life on the other hand would endow it with deeper significance, quality, and value. The ecological vision that a poetic insight engendered through the spiritual, would enhance all qualities of life and living, both in terms of the human and non-human. After all life becomes more meaningful when lived from with-in, more self-consciously, more deliberately, in perfect symphony with spiritual values – and the process of transformation is never exclusive but inclusive. In the final analysis the spiritual aesthetic of nature hastens in a life of quality and pure being, unbounded, unconditioned, but one conceived in difference and oneness at the same time.

Notes

1. An earlier version of this chapter was presented at a Conference on "Poetic Ecologies: Nature as Text and Text as Nature in English-Language Verse" in the Université Libre de Bruxelles, Belgium, in May 2008. Some portions of this essay have been translated into Romanian and published in *Post Modernism(e)* No 3-4, 2009; 69-84. Later the full text appeared in ISLE – Interdisciplinary Studies in Literature and Environment Vol. 18. Issue 2 (Spring 2011) pp. 302-322.
2. In his extremely perceptive analysis of the cultural and civilisational contexts of the present day world, *The Clash of Civilisations and the Remaking of World Order* (1996), Samuel P Huntington, has drawn attention to the historical postulate that in the post-Cold War world, culture is both a divisive and unifying force (p.28). He goes on to argue that "The polarisation of "East" and "West" culturally is in part another consequence of the universal but unfortunate practice of calling European civilisation Western civilisation. Instead of "East and West" it is more appropriate to speak of "the West and the rest" which at least implies the existence of many non-Wests." (p33). What I believe would be of significance in this observation is the recognition of non-homogeneous nature of culture which consequently identifies/validates difference and plurality, albeit not a self-defining one through the determinant of the West as a monolithic category. Ecocriticism in its essence recognises difference and heterogeneity.
3. Patrick D.Murphy, *Literature of Nature: An International Source Book* (Chicago: Fitzroy, 1998).

4. In this segment I have incorporated significant portions from my article entitled *Involution and Evolution: Some Conceptual Issues in the Contexts of Indian Discourses* that appeared in The *Trumpeter: Journal of Ecosophy*. Vol. 25, No.2 (2009).

5. To refer to the Indian *spiritual tradition* is not to deny the existence and significance of *materialist* discourses that have shaped the thinking of the people of India over the years. There has been a continued debate between the spiritual and the material as much as the theistic and the atheistic (see Debiprasad Chattopadyaya, DD Kosambi, Amartya Sen). However, the focus of my arguments is that Indian thought is *more concerned with seeking connections rather than insist on separateness*. This claim to connection does not preclude the value of existence and the individual.

6. There is little doubt that the rapid growth and development of ecology as a science and the corresponding emergence of ecologically sensitive critical theories in the social sciences and humanities is a propitious feature of the very idea that Nature is not merely there for the taking and neither is her resource unending. This definitely has political, economic, literary and aesthetic implications.

7. Amartya Sen, *The Argumentative Indian: Writings on Indian Culture, History and Identity* (Delhi: Penguin, 2005) p.25.

8. For a detailed discussion of the Vedic natural imagery and symbolism see OP Dwivedi, *Classical India*, in *A Companion to Environmental Philosophy*, ed Dale Jamieson (Malden: Blackwell, 2003)

9. *Human Ecology in the Vedas* (New Delhi: D K Printworld, 1999)

10. Sri Aurobindo* (1872-1950) was foremost among the nationalists who fought against the British Raj, a non-conformist and an activist aligned with the extremist Congressman, Bal Gangadhar Tilak, as opposed to the pacifist Mohandas Karamchand Gandhi. He wrote a great deal-ranging from violent nationalism through sociological treatises and political pamphlets to Yogic metaphysics and Vedic interpretation, poetics, prosody and history to psychological issues, literary criticism and mysticism. His major works include *The Foundations of Indian Culture, The Synthesis of Yoga, The Human Cycle, The Life Divine, Collected Poems, and Savitri: A Legend and a Symbol* (all published by the Ashram).

11. Sri Aurobindo, *The Future Poetry*, 2nd edn. Pondicherry: Sri Aurobindo Ashram, 1985. (1st edn:1953)

12. Hindu religious literature, the most ancient writings in the world, is of two types: primay scriptures (Sruti) and secondary scriptures (Smriti). The Sruti scriptures are of divine origin, whose truths were directly revealed to ancient rishis (sages) in their deep meditations. The Smriti scriptures are of human origin and were written to explain the Sruti writings and make them understandable and meaningful to the general population. Sruti scriptures include the four Vedas (Rig, Yajur, Sãma and Atharva) and the Bhagavad Gîtã, and constitute the highest religious authority in Hindu religion. Smriti

scriptures include five distinct groups of writings: Itihãsas (History or Epics), Purãnas (Mythology), Dharma Shãstras (Law Codes), Ãgamas & Tantras (Scriptures of various sects), Darshanas (Manuals of Philosophy – nyaya, vaisheshika, sankhya, yoga, mimasa and Vedanta).

13. Sri Aurobindo on Upanishads

14. *Savitri: A Legend and a Symbol.* Pondicherry: Sri Aurobindo Ashram, 1970. Sri Aurobindo (1872-1950) was foremost among the nationalists who fought against the British Raj, a non-conformist and an activist aligned with the extremist Congressman, Bal Gangadhar Tilak, as opposed to the pacifist Mohandas Karamchand Gandhi. He wrote a great deal – ranging from violent nationalism through sociological treatises and political pamphlets to Yogic metaphysics and Vedic interpretation., poetics, prosody and history to psychological issues, literary criticism and mysticism. His major works include *The Foundations of Indian Culture, The Synthesis of Yoga, The Human Cycle, The Life Divine, Collected Poems, and Savitri: A Legend and a Symbol (all published by the Ashram).*

15. In many ways Sri Aurobindo's systematic exploration of Involution and Evolution runs parallel to the thought of Pierre Teilhard de Chardin (1881-1955), the Jesuit Paleontologist, who attempted to combine his own scientific training in the Earth Sciences with the Christian metaphysics. Teilhard de Chardin is also credited with having even predicted the Internet. Contemporary philosophical debates have sort of rediscovered this "transhumanist" who engaged in a liberal dialogue with Christianity. Teilhard's notion of God as the Omega point toward which consciousness is evolving deserves special mention in this context.

16. Sri Aurobindo, Essays on the Gita, SABCL 13. Pondicherry Sri Aurobindo Ashram, 1970; p.452. Sri Aurobindo has also added a footnote to this observation: *This is from the point of view of our nature ascending upwards by self-conquest, effort, and discipline. There must also intervene more and more a descent of the divine Light, Presence and Power into the being to transform it; otherwise the change at the point of culmination and beyond it cannot take place. That is why there comes in as the last movement the necessity of an absolute self-surrender.* This can be seen as forming the basis of Sri Aurobindo's interpretation of the Gita as revealing essentially the power of Bhakti Yoga, and not merely *karma Yoga* and *jnana Yoga* as many others have seen in it.

17. *Aparardha*, "the lower half of world-existence", the hemisphere of the *triloka* (three worlds) of manas, pr ana, and anna or mind, life and matter. These three principles "are in themselves powers of the superior principles" of the higher hemisphere, *parardha.*

18. For a detailed discussion of the poem see my book *The Mantra of Vision.* Delhi: BR, 1997.

19. Sri Aurobindo, *The Life Divine.* 5th ed. (Pondicherry Sri Aurobindo Ashram, 1982; p 295). The term that he uses, *Consciousness-Force* is the Vedic equivalent of *Chit-Shakthi*, that is *self-aware energy.*

20. SABCL, XXVI, p.229.

21. O.P Dwivedi, "Classical India" *A Companion to Environmental Philosophy*, ed Dale Jamieson (Oxford: Blackwell, 2003) p.49.

Select Bibliography

Chapple, Christopher Key and Mary Evelyn Tucker, ed. *Hinduism and Ecology: The Intersection of Earth, Sky and Water*. Harvard: Harvard Univ. Press, 2000.

Dandekar, R.N. *Some Aspects of Vedic Exegesis*. Kuppuswami Sastri Birth-Centenary Commemoration Volume, Part II, ed. Janaki, S.S. Madras: The Kuppuswami Sastri Research Institute, 1985; 1-13.

Dwivedi, O.P. "Classical India" *A Companion to Environmental Philosophy*, ed Dale Jamieson. Oxford: Blackwell, 2003.

Huntington, Samuel P. *The Clash of Civilisations and the Remaking of World Order*. New Delhi: Penguin, 1997. (UK: Simon and Schuster, 1996)

Katz, Eric, Andrew Light and David Rothenberg, ed. *Beneath the Surface: Critical Essays in the Philosophy of Deep Ecology*. Cambridge: The MIT Press, 2000.

Macnaghten, Phil and John Urry, *Contested Natures*. London: Sage Publications, 1998.

Murali, S. *Rediscovering the Roots of Eco-Consciousness*, Summerhill, VII, 1 & 2, Summer-Winter, 2001, 16-18

Murali,S. *Ecological Wisdom and Alter/native Discourses: Some Aspects of Spatio-Temporal Awareness in Ancient Indian Culture with special Reference to South India,* Summerhill, VIII,2, Winter 2002, 8-12.

Murali, S. *The Mantra of Vision*. Delhi: BR, 1997.

Murali,S and Usha VT. *Tradition and Terrain: Aesthetic Continuities*. Delhi: BR Publishing Corporation, 2006.

Murali, S. Ed. *Nature and Human Nature: Literature, Ecology, Meaning*. New Delhi: Prestige, 2009.

Murphy, Patrick D. *Literature of Nature: An International Source Book. Chicago: Fitzroy*, 1998.

Prabhavananda, Swami. *The Spiritual Heritage of India*. Madras: Sri Ramakrishna Math, 1981.

Shah, Ramesh Chandra. *Ancestral Voices: Reflections on Vedic, Classical and Bhakti Poetry*. Delhi: Motilal Banarsidass Publishers, 2006. [first published by The Temenos Akademy, UK, 2001]

Simmons, IG. *Interpreting Nature: Cultural Constructions of the Environment*, London & NY: Routledge, 1993.

Sen, Amartya. *The Argumentative Indian: Writings on Indian Culture, History and Identity*. Delhi: Penguin, 2005.

Sri Aurobindo, *Essays on the Gita*, SABCL 13. Pondicherry: Sri AurobindoAshram, 1970.

Sri Aurobindo, *The Life Divine*. 5th ed. Pondicherry: Sri Aurobindo Ashram, 1982.

Sri Aurobindo, *Savitri: A Legend and a Symbol.* Pondicherry: Sri Aurobindo Ashram, 1970.

Sri Aurobindo, *The Secret of the Veda. 3rd ed.* Pondicherry: Sri AurobindoAshram, 1971.

Steinhart, Eric. "Teilhard de Chardin and Transhumanism." *Journal of Evolution and Technology,* Vol 20 Issue 1- December 2008; 1-22.

Vannucci, Marta. *Human Ecology in the Vedas.* New Delhi: D K Printworld, 1999.

CHAPTER 4

Savitri – Mahakavya

To read Sri Aurobindo's poem *Savitri* is to witness a tremendous adventure in the interior realms; to witness and participate in a multidimensional quest. It is perhaps the best example of spiritual poetry, poetry as *dhyana mantra.* Sri Aurobindo's *magnum opus* is an Indian epic, a *mahakavya.*

Sri Aurobindo developed certain specific spiritual practices that afforded him experiences in the interior spaces of the soul – and his long poem *Savitri* constitutes an evocative multidimensional map of such transformative encounters. Running into 12 books and 49 cantos, *Savitri* is the longest poem in the English language and the poet consistently worked on it for close to five decades. Taking off from a small anecdote in the Mahabharata, this poem is cast as a legend and a symbol – the entire text is an unfolding of the image of aesthetic transformation in symbolic terms.

Sri Aurobindo, as we have seen, was a prolific writer whose work ranged from political pamphlets to sociological treatises, exegesis on the Vedas, the Upanishads and the Bhagavad Gita, to systematic treatises on yoga and its various dimensions, from critical thinking on the foundations of Indian culture and history to philosophical writings on the meaning of spiritual being and the poetics of spiritual transformation.

According to him *all life is yoga* – the integration of inner and outer nature – a union that would progressively *spiritualise* all being. In philosophical terms, consciousness *is* 'everything that exists' and there is a gradual evolution from the material (the *inconscient* state in Aurobindian terminology) to that of being gradually and systematically self-conscious and spiritually 'superconscient' (a state above the consciousness). He designated specific hierarchies of the mind such as 'Higher Mind', 'Illumined Mind', 'Intuition' and 'Overmind' – stages to be reached before achieving the complete divinisation of all being (matter inclusive), in the 'Supramental' being.

Poetry, as he saw it, worked as an index of the evolving consciousness.

The poem revolves round the symbolic dimensions of its characters and their experiences. The tale of Satyavan and Savitri is simple enough. The king of Madra, Aswapathy, has a daughter Savitri, who falls in love with the Salwa prince, Satyavan, the son of a dispossessed and blind king Dyumatsena. It is foretold that Satyavan is to die within a year of their marriage. Savitri is undaunted and they are married. When Satyavan dies at the destined time, Savitri awaits Yama (the lord of death) to come and possess his soul. She follows the soul into the nether realms. Despite her repeated requests, Yama is unrelenting in granting her the life of Satyavan. Nevertheless, she persists and is finally able to overcome death with her perseverance and single-minded commitment. Satyavan is finally reunited with Savitri in an eternal life of happiness.

The text of *Savitri* is replete with unique instances of the power of the word from its very opening. Here is how the poet depicts the slow movement of the trio – Satyavan, Death, and Savitri – into the realms of the beyond:

> Luminous he moved away; behind him Death
> Went slowly with his noiseless tread, as seen
> In dream-built fields a shadowy herdsman glides
> Behind some wanderer from his voiceless herds,
> And Savitri moved behind eternal Death,
> Her mortal pace was equalled with the god's.
> Wordless she travelled in her lover's steps,
> Planting her human feet where his had trod,
> Into the perilous silences beyond. (IX.i.211–19)

The mantra, or the highest intensity of poetic expression, according to Sri Aurobindo, is reached when sound and sense (sabda and artha) combine in the right order, as it happens in the following instance where the nuances of the language are captured:

> Only sometimes small thoughts rose and fell
> Like quiet waves upon a silent sea
> Or ripples passing over a lonely pool
> When a stray stone disturbs its dreaming rest. (VII. vi.405–08)

And again:

> As blooms a flower in an unvisited place
> The wide world knew not yet the inhabitant flame,
> Yet something deeply stirred and dimly knew;
> There was a movement and a passionate call,

A rainbow dream, a hope of golden change;
Some secret wing of expectation beat,
A growing sense of something new and rare
And beautiful stole across the heart of time. (IV. ii.289–96)

To read *Savitri* is indeed to witness a tremendous adventure in the interior realms, to witness and participate in a multidimensional quest ranging beyond the visible and the tangible. And because *Savitri* is cast in the mould of epic poetry, *mahakavya* – as this chapter endeavours to show – the requisite state of mind is one of openness and humility similar to that of prayer. It is desired that as we read, each word and each phrase should ring in a 'solitude and an immensity', heard in the 'listening spaces of the soul,' in the 'inner acoustic space', and seized by the deeper self, when the mantric evocations come into effect ("*Srotrasya srotram*" (*Kena Upanishad*, 1.2) We will also see how Sri Aurobindo integrates word and meaning in the process of reaching out to the immense possibilities of mantra or mahavakya, the sequence of mantra.

'*To embellish life with beauty*', writes Sri Aurobindo in *The Future Poetry*, 'is only the most outward function of art and poetry, to make life more intimately beautiful and noble and great and full of meaning is its higher office, but its highest comes when the poet becomes the seer and reveals to man his eternal self and the godheads of its manifestation" (243). And this highest function is what he has achieved in this work.

Scholars and academics have classified Sri Aurobindo's *Savitri* as an epic. In this chapter, we shall explore the Indian idea of *Mahakavya* and examine *Savitri* as *Mahakavya*. To begin with, there are these two broad categories in this term – *Maha* or *Mahat* and *Kavya* or poetry. Let us take these up one by one.

Mahat

Mahat relates to the notion of grand or great as we understand it in *Mahabharatham* or *Mahaprastanam*. Mahat also connotes a certain state of consciousness in the spiritual realms. The Upanishads teach that there are three distinct states of consciousness from the perception of the human self.

The first is the *waking state* characterised by the awareness of things external to the body. And in this state of awareness the human being is referred to as *vaiswanara*, because he/she is then "lord of the physical body". The second is the dreaming state – *taijasa* – and this is the condition intermediate between waking and deep sleep. The mind is now active, independently of the sense organs, and in this state the human being is a purely mental being. The third state is that of deep sleep – known as *prajna* – when the human being is unaware of both external and the internal worlds. There is a fourth transcendental state – *turiya* –the state of pure consciousness. As we read in the Mandukya Upanishad:

> The fourth is not subjective experience, nor objective experience, nor experience intermediate between the two, nor is it a negative condition which is neither consciousness nor unconsciousness. It is not the knowledge of the senses, nor is it relative knowledge, nor yet inferential knowledge. Beyond the senses, beyond the understanding, beyond all expression is the Fourth. It is pure unitary consciousness, wherein awareness of the world and of multiplicity is completely obliterated.[1]

Turiya, the final all-embracing goal of the spiritual life, is sometimes conceived by the Upanishads as a state of knowledge, sometimes as a state of liberation. Now, as for knowledge there is this distinction between *Para Vidya* and *Apara Vidya* – the higher and the lower. The lower is the knowledge afforded by the Vedas, and would include other levels of phonology, grammar, syntax, etymology, meter and astronomy. This is Apara Vidya. The Para Vidya is knowledge of that by which one knows the Brahman, the changeless reality. Knowledge of the atman is also para vidya. This path toward self-realisation is also recognised by the Puranas. Mahat occurs in the Puranas where the lokas or worlds fall into a sevenfold classification – Bhur, Bhuvar, Swar, Mahar, Jana, Tapa and Satya. Hence the idea of knowledge and liberation.

In the *Vishnu Purana*, the rishi Parasara explains to Maitreya about the transitory realms of *Bhur, Bhuvar, Swar*, and the higher realms of *Jana, Tapa, Satya*. The *Maharloka* occurs in between the two realms. In Sri Aurobindo's scheme, Matter, Life, and Mind constitute the lower order and from there on, in the hierarchical scheme of consciousness, the *Overmental Realms* commence. There are then over-the-mental states, the Higher Mind, Illumined Mind, Intuition, and the Overmind. The *Supermind* is *Vijnanaloka*, or Maharloka, and occurs as the intermediary transitional plane between the *Parardha,* the Upper hemisphere of three higher worlds –Sat, Chit, Ananda– and the *Aparardha*, the lower hemisphere of world existence – Mind, Life, and Matter. Hence Maharloka approximates to the Supermind. At each transition of the world-ascent, from matter to life, from life to mind, from mind bound to free intelligence, as the latent, half-manifested or already manifest soul rises to a higher and higher level of being, the nature also is elevated into a superior working, a wider consciousness, a vaster force and an intenser or larger range and joy of existence. But the transition from the mind-self to the knowledge-self is the great and the decisive transition in the Yoga. It is the shaking off of the last hold on us of the cosmic ignorance and our firm foundation in the truth of things, in a consciousness infinite and eternal and inviolable by obscurity, falsehood, suffering or error[2]. In *Savitri* Sri Aurobindo has endeavoured to approximate to the utterances of the overmental levels – that is where the word and vision fuse into one another, a sort of space-time of integrated meaning. Of course in a long poem of such a massive scale it is not possible to maintain the highest intensity of poetic speech throughout, but in certain places we do get brief glimpses of the Maharloka, when the word and vision fuse together to effect the rending of the veil.

Savitri is perhaps the longest epic available in the English language. The epic written and rewritten in several pages, some copied, some written down by several hands while the master recited, the final text incorporating innumerable corrections and emendations still reads like one complete text interspaced with wealth of interior details and accounts of yoga and metaphysics – which far exceeds in detail anything else on a similar scale – and has survived generations. Sri Aurobindo is supposed to have begun work on it a long time ago even before he reached Pondicherry and he went on reworking and editing till his passing. The first Canto itself appears to have gone through thirteen close-readings and emendations according to textual scholarship available. The earliest known manuscript is dated 1916. Part one of the first edition was published in 1950.

To my knowledge there is only another long epic in a similar scale – but that comes to us English translation from the original Greek: Nikos Kazantzakis's *Odyssey a Modern Sequel*, translated by Kimon Friar, which runs into 33,333 lines. The German poet Goethe had also meticulously worked on his *Faust*, and the Italian poet, Dante at his *Divine Comedy*, but never to such a scale!

According to Sri Aurobindo *Savitri* was not a poem to be completed and finished. *He used the poem as a means of ascension...* [3]

> *Savitri* began as a narrative poem of moderate length based on a legend told in the Mahabharata. Sri Aurobindo considered the story to be originally "one of the many symbolic myths of the Vedic cycle". Bringing

out its symbolism and charging it progressively with his own spiritual vision, he turned *Savitri* into the epic it is today. By the time it was published, some passages had gone through dozens of drafts. Sri Aurobindo explained how he wrote the poem: *"I used Savitri as a means of ascension. I began with it on a certain mental level, each time I could reach a higher level I rewrote from that level... In fact Savitri has not been regarded by me as a poem to be written and finished, but as a field of experimentation to see how far poetry could be written from one's own yogic consciousness and how that could be made creative".*

The following outline of the composition and publication of *Savitri* draws upon existing manuscripts and other textual materials, supplemented by the author's letters on the poem. In brief, *Savitri* took shape through three major phases.

Before 1920, Sri Aurobindo made a number of drafts of a narrative poem retelling in an original way the tale of Savitri and Satyavan. Its last version had a plan of eight books in two parts; the books were not divided into cantos. In the 1930s, he set about converting this narrative poem into an epic. For a long time he concentrated on the description of Aswapati's Yoga prior to the birth of Savitri, creating by 1945 a new – Part One – with three books and many cantos. In the last phase, besides revising Part One for publication, he reworked and enlarged most of the books written in the first period. He added a book on the Yoga of Savitri, making twelve books and forty-nine cantos in all and completing Parts Two and Three.

Now, as we have it in the present after editions and emendations is in the form of an epic. It is subtitled, *A Legend and a Symbol. It runs into twelve books:*

1. The book of beginnings
2. The book of the Traveler of the Worlds
3. The book of the Divine Mother
4. The book of the Birth and Quest
5. The book of Love
6. The book of Fate
7. The book of Yoga
8. The book of Death
9. The book of Eternal Night
10. The book of the Double Twilight
11. The book of everlasting day
12. Epilogue

The overall structure of the poem and its thematic outline would reveal the intense effort and endeavor the poet has undertaken in order to approximate to the idea of mahakavya. Over and above this, there are several aspects of Sri Aurobindo's spiritual theories that also serve to give a unique structure to the poem. The poem has been used as a tool for spiritual guidance for meditation and integral yoga. Innumerable scholars have written and explicated this long poem in their own unique manner and from their levels of understanding – we have the unique textual explications and interior corroborations of A B Purani, M P Pandit, Srinivasa Iyengar, Prema Nandakumar, Sisir Kumar Ghose, P Lal, Haridas Choudhury, Kishore Gandhi, Shankar Mokashi-Punekar, Rohit Mehta and several insightful scholars like these who have read and analysed each and every line for the sake of the ardent devotee who approaches the poem as an aid to meditation and self-evolution. And of course the Mother has held several conversations on the poem. Some like P Lal have been derogative, for their own advantage (of course solely in an academic manner). CD Narasimhaiah, the doyen of Comparative literary aesthetics in Indian Universities started off as an ardent anti-Aurobindonian, and eventually has after several readings, debates, lectures, seminars and workshops, admitted, with reference to *Savitri*, if poetry is *dhyana mantra* you find it here! [But this not to make us relax deeper into our chairs and nod away as if this is a forgone conclusion! It is perhaps an incentive to read the poem again and again and respond to it with the seriousness that the poet intended!]

In general, C.D. Narasimhaiah, has classified the reader of a literary or aesthetic work like this: *Acharya* – the cultivated reader; *Pundita* – the learned one, but not necessarily a discriminating one; *Bhakta* – the devoted reader – devoted to the writer, the cause; *Sadharanajana* – the common reader and *Alpabuddhijana* – the groundling, of "little intelligence" [4]In our reading of this great epic we cannot be like the last two! We have to recognise the *mahat* aspect of this poem, in all its levels. And in my rereading I would like to highlight the structural, aesthetic and thematic significance of the poem which makes it a mahakavya.

Kavya

Now we come to the poetry or Kavya part. Indian scholars had generally designated literature as that *which is seen* (*drisya*, on stage) and that which is heard (*sravya*, through literature). Although poetry (kavya) is an all-inclusive term, theatre had developed suitably early in this country. The oldest extant text on dramaturgy in India is Bharata's *Natyasastra.* This treatise is a comprehensive account of everything from ritual preliminaries of a theatrical performance to the various types of acting (language, gestures, facial expressions, costume and makeup) to music, dance and stage design, clearly addressed to those who create and perform drama. The 6th Chapter in the *Natyasastra*, is the closest thing we have to a foundational text of the discipline of aesthetics, where the celebrated aphorism on rasa occurs. Rasa is produced from a combination of Determinants (vibhava), Consequents (anubhava) and Transitory States (vyabhicaribhava)[5]. As Bharata sees it, rasa arises from conjunction of *vibhava, anubhava and vyabhicharibhava* – factors, reactions and transitory emotions.

Rasa has come to be looked upon as the soul of poetics. There have been several schools of Sanskrit aestheticians who have put forward various aspects of significance that would designate the essence of poetry and poetics. The word, the manner and style of its composition, the alankaras or ornamentation, the subtleties of the narrative, the gunas and doshas of composition, their manner and mode of origin and reception, the resonance and tone – all these aspects and more have been the bone of contention in their hair-splitting analysis of the poetic. Each school has had its own spokespersons and theoreticians, however, the idea of rasa apparently have successfully continued to survive and prevail. In terms of the conceptual clarity of idea, its reach and magnitude, its trace – there is no such all-inclusive terminological equivalent to the notion of rasa. It is multidimensional in its aesthetic circuit that includes the creator, the created and the reader/spectator. Raso vai sah, says the Taittiriya Upanishad. Rasa is that which exists, bliss, verily is the essence of existence.

Now, in terms of its structure and form, Kavya is further categorised into:

(i) Mahakavya, long poems structured into chapters, following all the prescribed regulations of classical poetry; and,

(ii) Laghu-kavya, shorter poems or poetry of the minor form.

Bhamaha and Vamana describe these forms as *Nibaddha* (cohesive poetry) and *a-nibaddha* (non-cohesive poetry). Nibaddha which is equated with Mahakavya includes both the long poems (in verse, prose or a mixture of the two champu) as also Drama. a-nibaddha equated with Laghu-kavya covers all kinds of short poems say of one or two stanzas.

Specifying the characteristics of a *Mahakavya*, Bhamaha wrote that the epic is divided into cantos, its subject is profound with its hero being great or characterised by quiet gallantry and loftiness of conduct. Its language is witty, its story is devoid of unnecessary elements or matter and in spite of being rhetorical, it is based on morality. Thus in Bhamaha's view the important elements of an Epic are–

An epic is divided into Cantos
It deals with a great and profound subject
The action revolves round a Sublime hero
The epic would interpret the four levels of dharma, 'artha, kama and moksha
The rise of the hero
The epic holds up the element of righteousness
Dramatic characteristic -Five divisions
Inclusion of nature of people and various sentiments
Prosperity- Descriptions of Moonrise, Seasons etc.[6]

According to Dandin, *Mahakavya* is a creation divided in to cantos. It contains words of benediction, praise or greetings and outline of the story at the beginning. The subject of an epic is historical or based on the real story of a gentleman. It contains the description of sublime, virtuous, clever hero's attainment of four human pursuit's viz. Virtue, Wealth, Sensual pleasures and Salvation. It contains the description of a city, ocean, mountain, season, moonrise, sun-rise, and garden, messenger, marching and rising of the hero. It includes dalliance, intoxication, and enjoyment of love, separation, marriage and birth of a son. It has mantra, messenger, marching and rising of the hero.

The *Mahakavya* is enriched with rhetoric, extensive and aesthetic and emotional content. The Cantos should not be comprehensive; story must contain interesting events and should include elements like description of twilight, there must be a change of meter at the end of the Canto. The *Mahakavya* containing the above characteristics serves the popular interest and has lasting effect till the end of an era.

Formally speaking, Mahakavya contains a productive or non-productive poetic story. It may contain interludes or intermediary stories, whose objective is to give multiple dimensions to the main story. *Mahakavya* is divided into Cantos and contains a story full of dramatic elements. It depicts the entire life and it contains a heroic deed or any important incident. The poet builds up the story based on this incident with rhetoric description, illustration of Nature and different worldly and divine depictions. The mundane descriptions include that of Nature, garden and city, while the divine includes description of Gods and heaven. The hero of a *Mahakavya* is born as a virtuous person, meritorious, perhaps, no less than a warrior, desirous of conquering the whole world. He is powerful, sagacious, and a tactful King. (There is strategically no gender divide that we can note here) *Mahakavya* will have a villain and description about his lineage. It depicts victory of the hero and defeat of the villain. As Sanskrit aestheticians see it, Mahakavya necessarily connects with the idea of *Dharma.* As it is generally understood, Mahakavya is usually an elaborate epic in the courtly style – or kavya in classic style – strung round a strong narrative element (kathavastu) of sublime characters spread over several cantos (Sarga-bandha) adorned with eighteen types of descriptions (*ashta-dasha-varnana*), with well-chosen forms (guna) of expression, syntax, and graces of rasa and beauty (alankara) and endowed with eloquent imagination; and, at the same time, satisfying all the norms and principles (kavya-lakshana) prescribed for the epic by the Kavya-shastra texts. Apart from these, it must needs necessarily promote and further the cause of the *Dharma.*[7]

Dandin in his *Kavyadarsa* gives an elaborate definition of Mahakavya, the summit of Kavya genre: the composition in Cantos (Sargabandha) begins with a benediction (Mangala), or a salutation or an indication of the plot. It is based on a traditional narrative, or on a true event from one or the other sources. It deals with the fruits of the four aims of life (chatur-vidha phala Purushartha)[8] Its hero is skillful and noble (dhirodatta), adorned (alamkara) with eighteen (ahsta-dasha varnana) types of descriptions including that of cities (nagara), oceans (sagara), mountains (shaila), seasons (vasantadi ritu), the rising/setting of sun and moon(chandra-surya udaya – asthamana), playing in pleasure-parks (vana vihara), (udyana), and in water (jala krida), drinking parties and the delights of love-making (madyapana surata), weddings (vivaha), srngara (vipralamba) the separation of lovers (viraha), discussions with the wise [see the presence of old wise saints] the birth of a son (putrodaya), state-craft (raja-mantra), gambling or sending messengers (dyuta), wars (yuddha), campaigns (jaitra-yatra), and accomplishments of the hero (nayaka abyudaya); not too condensed; pervaded with Rasa (aesthetic mood) and Bhava (basic emotion); with Cantos that are not overly diffuse, in meters that are pleasing to hear, with proper junctures, and ending with different meters (that is, meters different from the main or the carrying meter of the Canto); such a Kavya pleasing to the world and well ornamented (Sadalamkriti) will last until the end of creation. Even if it lacks some of these features, a Kavya does not become bad, if the perfection of the things that are present delights the connoisseurs (Sahrdaya)." Viswanatha has pointed out that a mahakavya is a unique instance of a combination of Mahavakyas, or outstanding statements.

In general now, we can conclude, the epic plot centers around a Hero of Unbelievable Stature. The epic hero completes what other people might only attempt to do. In ancient epics, the hero often is either partially divine or at least protected by a god or God. Any significant epic often involves deeds of superhuman strength and valor. The hero accomplishes feats no ordinary human could even attempt. The epic calls for a Vast Setting. The action spans not only geographical but also often cosmological space: across land, sea, into the underworld, or thru space or time etc. The epic involves supernatural and-or otherworldly forces – Gods, demons, angels, time/space travel, cheating death etc. The language of the epic reflects a sustained elevation of style. Perhaps they would appear to be *overwritten.* The epic Poet remains objective and omniscient. The narrator sees and knows all and presents all perspectives in the round. In brief, the Epic reflects a Cognitive or Spiritual Model of human Development. Beginning with Gilgamesh and continuing on through *Achilles, Odysseus, Beowulf* and *Sir Gawain* – not to mention Hollywood's own Superman, Spiderman and Batman or The Hulk – the very soul of the epic culminates around the hero's journey of self-discovery and emotional/psychological/spiritual maturation. Perhaps, all epics seem to start with the *ur-hero*, Gilgamesh's journey to involve the hero: confronting the reality of death and thus realising heroism as a spiritual or psychological quality, not just a physical one. This is the archetypal hero, the savior of all mankind. The epical narrative involves a journey toward the nether world below the earth, to the underworld, where death itself abides, only to learn that love is more valuable than material wealth or life itself. This is true of all Mahakavyas. *Savitri* is no exception, the integration of the themes of love, death and rebirth reverberate in its structure; but the levels of the legend and symbol bring forth a different dimension to the narrative. Here in its context there is the unfolding of two magnificent interior journeys – one of Aswapathy and the other of *Savitri* – a journey that desires and involves the transformation of all mankind. The space of *Savitri* is bracketed within the space of two dawns – from dawn to a superdawn – a mega effort endeavouring a supramental transformation:

> All now is changed, yet all is still the same.
> Lo, we have looked upon the face of God,
> Our life has opened with divinity.
> We have borne identity with the Supreme
> And known his meaning in our mortal lives.
> Our love has grown greater by that mighty touch
> And learned its heavenly significance,
> Yet nothing is lost of mortal love's delight.
> Heaven's touch fulfils but cancels not our earth:
> Our bodies need each other in the same last;
> Still in our breasts repeat heavenly secret rhythm
> Our human heart-beats passionately close.
> Still am I she who came to thee mid the murmur
> Of sunlit leaves upon this forest verge;
> I am the Madran, I am Savitri.
> All that I was before, I am to thee still,
> Close comrade of thy thoughts and hopes and toils,
> All happy contraries I would join for thee.
> All sweet relations marry in our life;
> I am thy kingdom even as thou art mine,
> The sovereign and the slave of thy desire...

The final realisation– from the dawn to a greater dawn:

> "Awakened to the meaning of my heart
> That to feel love and oneness is to live
> And this the magic of our golden change,
> Is all the truth I know or seek, O sage."

Savitri is a long narrative about *a serious or worthy traditional subject*, falling in line with the mahakavya tradition, structurally and thematically. Its diction is elevated in style. It employs a formal, dignified, objective tone and affords several figures of speech. As defined by the concept of Mahakavya, the narrative is focused on the exploits of *the epic hero or demigod who represents the cultural values of a race, nation, or religious group*. In fact there are two heroes – Aswapathy whose exploits are covered in the earlier part and Savitri, whose yoga is described in the latter half. It is decreed that the hero's success or failure determines the fate of an entire people or nation – this is quite true in the context of *Savitri.* The action does take place in a vast setting, on a cosmic scale; it covers a wide geographic area – the realms explored are overmental and cosmic. The context of the poem falls beyond human history. The action explored contains superhuman feats of strength beyond that of any military prowess. The overhang of supernatural intervention often implies two or more simultaneous plots – as defined by the idea of Mahakavya. This is also the case with *Savitri.*

The poem begins with the invocation of a symbolic dawn a formal prayer appropriate to the structure of a Mahakavya. The narrative starts in *medias res*, in the middle of the action. Subsequently, the earlier events leading up to the start of the poem are recounted in the characters' narratives or in flashbacks. The epic usually contains long catalogues of heroes or important characters, focusing on highborn kings and great warriors rather than peasants and commoners. The epic employs extended similes (called epic similes) at appropriate spots of the story, and a traditional scene of extended description in which the hero arms himself. This is also quite true in the context of *Savitri.* Often, the main protagonist undergoes a terrifying journey – sometimes a descent into the underworld – i.e., into hell or the realm of the dead. As mentioned earlier, both Aswapathy and Savitri undertake this sort of superhuman journey. Thus, even any cursory glance at this list of requisites one can say that *Savitri* maintains the rigidity of the epic in terms of structure and aesthesis. It is Mahakavya in the light of the Indian aesthetic theories. *Savitri* of course fits in with all these requirements of *Mahakavya.* In terms of structure and aesthetic – the formal and thematic – the poem falls in line with all the great Mahakavyas. It maintains a grandiose narrative and deals with the spiritual planes of existence. This is not to overstate this point and take it to its extreme limits. The epic appears to occur on its own initiative – it is part of the creative destiny of humankind. Here and elsewhere, I have looked upon the idea of epic and mahakavya as mutually interchangeable concepts, because I hold the belief that cultural and historical differences apart, the idea of the epic from mythical times coincides with the idea of the mahakavya. We see this in the context of *Savitri* – albeit couched in the idiom of the colonial, with clear overtones of the nineteenth century narratives, the poem runs deep roots in the Indic tradition.

Comparing the apocalyptic visionaries Dante and Sri Aurobindo, in *The Divine Comedy* and *Savitri*, Prema Nandakumar has noted:

> The compulsion behind the structure of Dante's journey into Hell, Purgatory and Paradiso, is the love that saves man, the love that moves the sun and the stars, an intense love for God. For a sinner like him, the love he bore for Beatrice alone returns to him as the saving grace, which first sends Virgil to lead him through Hell and Purgatory. "A worthier spirit", Beatrice, is to lead Dante through Paradise. Being led by the invisible love and visible company of Beatrice through the triple worlds is the main vision in *The Divine Comedy*.
>
> For Sri Aurobindo's *Savitri* too, the basis was the vision of a descending Grace that was vouchsafed to him in the course of his yoga.[9]

A "world's desire" compelled the mortal birth of Savitri, and the poet embarks on a journey into the interior realms, in the wake of love and death. This process is the epical recovery of word and deed which is a beyonding of memory and dream, history and myth. Here's what the Mother of the Sri Aurobindo Ashram says about *Savitri:*

- "*Savitri*, is this prophetic vision of the world's history, including the announcement of the earth's future." (from the *introduction to Meditations on Savitri*, vol. 1, 1964)
- "The importance of *Savitri* is immense. Its subject is universal. Its revelation is prophetic. The time spent in its atmosphere is not wasted." (from the message for the *Meditations on Savitri* exhibition, 1967)
- She wrote that *Savitri* is: "The daily record of the spiritual experiences of the individual who has written." "a complete system of yoga which can serve as a guide for those who want to follow the integral sadhana." "*The yoga of the Earth in its ascension towards the Divine*."
- VAK – Mantra – In *Savitri* mahakavya what he is doing is to approximate to that act of reaching after the right word – charged inspiration and expression

We are reminded of Bhamaha's statement: *sabdartha sahitam kavyam* – a poem is a combination of *sabda (sound)* and *artha* (meaning). When the combination is effectively carried out the mantra is accomplished. In a superhuman reaching after the mantra, the legend is transmuted into the symbol.

Let us now briefly examine the Vedic connection. As we have already seen, the Vedic vision (a poetic vision that informs the foundations of later Indian belief structures) of life itself is cyclical as an extension of the order of nature (the Vedic poets structured their thought in terms of *Chhandas*, or universal rhythm). These motifs and views of life as ritual and the self itself as an offering have survived as symbolic rituals and celebratory acts even up to the present (albeit with a few changes as they are upheld by Brahmanical rites and practices.) These ideas get elaborated in the manner in which the mantras – spiritually codified incantations – are chanted, and also in the use of specific materials and forms of ritualistic worship.

The Vedas have been seen as secular narratives encompassing the pastoral vision of the ancient people of the Indo-Gangetic plains in a poetic mould. Many insightful scholars have also perceived in the Vedic mantras a symbolic structure that provides them with an outer exoteric order and an inner esoteric meaning which makes sense only to the initiated. The Upanishads which followed in their wake are the intellectual renderings or philosophical speculations branching off from those codes.

Sri Aurobindo has delved deep into the Vedic texts (translated and edited some mandalas), and explicated some of the Upanishads.

Let us quickly go through these to get our bearings correct. Eventually aesthetic theorising in the wake of the Vedic and Upanishadic tradition and the innumerable *desi* or little traditions and aesthetic practices, commenced roughly with the 1st cent. There have been a continuous narrative and argumentative tradition in Sanskrit aesthetics as insightful critics have shown us. Sri Aurobindo was an extraordinary scholar of ancient, medieval, Victorian and to a certain extent the early modernist aesthetic. His insights have been shaped by what he read, analysed and absorbed. He was a proliferous writer as all of us know already. His works range from poetry to philosophy, to political treatises to sociological theorising, translations from Greek, Sanskrit, and which include key texts from several Indian languages, to exegesis on Vedic and Upanishadic texts. His interpretations of Yogic systems and the text of the Gita are extraordinary. My argument is that we need to approach the work of a poet who gathered innumerable perceptions and insights from a wealth cultures and continents with the same scale of gravity and seriousness. *Savitri* is not a poem to be read and forgotten, but it needs to be chewed and digested– it is not a functional text but integral to the entire enterprise. This is the reason why we look upon it as a mahakavya.

The Vedic traditions designate *antaschamatkara–* spiritual expression as the prime purpose of poetry. And its excellence consists in its effective deploying of the occult ranges and their presence as actual felt experiences of sight and sound, and remaining intensely spiritual even in sequences that are not directly linked with spirituality.

In an early essay – *The Strength of Stillness* – Sri Aurobindo writes of the two great forces in the universe, silence and speech, and relates them to action in the world:

> When we strive to act, the forces of Nature do their will with us; when we grow still, we become their master.... The more complete the calm, the mightier the yogic power, the greater the force in action.

And the limits of action reach overt inaction and touch upon the deep roots of being. Here the access to the self-sustaining harmony of the Spirit begins, and all contraries and differences cease to be. Much later he writes:

> When something expresses perfectly what it was meant to express, the completeness brings with it a sense of harmony, a sense of artistic perfection; it gives even to what is discordant a place in a system of cosmic concordances and the discords become part of a vast harmony, and wherever there is harmony, there is a sense of beauty.

Action, silence, harmony and beauty – form the cornerstones of the aesthetic resolution that Sri Aurobindo drives towards conceptually. And it is out of a source of austere stillness that he seeks the will to supramental transformation. We read in one of his letters: In my view a man's value does not depend on what he learns or his position or fame, or what he does but on what he is and inwardly becomes. And this inward becoming is the creative self, becoming conscious of its spiritual affinities. In the Aurobindian scheme of things poetry "opens a passage between the external consciousness and the inner mind or vital... And, this it achieves through the surrender to the avesa from the above-mental planes – it is an inrush and overflow to the level of ananda. *Apare kavyasamsare kavireva prajapatih – in the wonderful world of poetry, the poet is the prajapati."*

Vagvai brahmedi, says the Upanishad. The word is brahman. Yaska (Ca. 5th-6th BCE), the Etymologist of the ancient India, describes Vak (speech) as the divine gift to humans in order to clearly express their thoughts (*devim vacam ajanayanta*- Nirukta. 11.29); and, he terms the purified articulate speech as *Paviravi* – sharp as the resonance (*tanyatu*) of the thunderbolt which originates from an invisible power. (*Tad devata vak paviravi. paviravi cha divya Vac tanyatus tanitri vaco'nyasyah* – Nirukta. 12.30).[10]

While explaining the relation between Vac and consciousness in the *Brhadaranyaka Upanishad*, Yajnavalkya says that Vak is a form of expression of consciousness. And, he argues, there could be no speech without consciousness. However, Consciousness does not directly act upon the principle of speech; but it operates through intermediary organs and the breath to deliver speech.

In the light of Sri Aurobindo's vision which corresponds to the Vedic, the rhythms of cosmic vibrations issue forth from four levels which correspond to the various levels in manifestation:

> *Para-Vak* is the highest form of sound. It issues forth from the Supernal Ether (*paramam vyomam*) where all the sound vibrations that build the various worlds pre-exist in an undifferentiated state.

Pashyanti is the sound vibration heard in the Causal worlds. Pashyanti in Sanskrit means "seeing speech". A sage whose consciousness is concentrated in the causal body is able to "glimpse" a Truth in a vision or a revelation. Knowledge is acquired in the inner mind by sight without the use of the reasoning faculty or sensory data.

Madhyama (Middle) is the sound as perceived in the subtle or the Pranic world. A good example of this would be the thought-forms held in our mind.

Vaikhari is the lowest form of sound and it signifies outward expression. This is the spoken word emerging from the throat and vocalised.

Mahakavya and mahavakya. Viswanatha in his *Sahityadarpanam* instances Mahakavya as a combination of many *mahavakya.* In the space of the mahakavya all words become *chandas*, all expression becomes the mantra.

For Sri Aurobindo, all poetry is inspiration-- a thing breathed into the thinking organ from above; it is recorded in the mind, but is born in the higher principle of direct knowledge or ideal vision which surpasses the mind. It is in reality a revelation.

This is the process of poetry as he visualised it: Vision– Inspiration – Revelation. Revelation pertains to the discovery of that inner and deeper vision that the human mind can afford, and inspiration brings down the corresponding word. The ideal combination is the merging of vision and word – and this leads to the ultimate unity – the mantra.

In fact the Aurobindian idea of poetry is as the *mantra of vision.*[11] For him, all art in its own way seeks to arrive at a concentrated expression of the spirit, and it is from the Soul that the expression originates and it is to the Soul that it unveils the Real. Soul is the aesthetic being the *antaratman.*[12] In the final analysis Sri Aurobindo's poetry is poetry of self-recovery and self-revelation. As poetry itself is an index of the evolving human consciousness, its realms are within the human's being. As he finely frames it in one of his sonnets:

> In us too Krishna seeks for love and joy,
> In us too Shiva struggles with the world's grief.
> One Self in all of us endures annoy,
> Cries in his pain and asks his fate's relief.[13]

Sri Aurobindo's works reveal this inner struggle of the self for a complete revelation, his poetry and poetics form one comprehensive whole, where vision, inspiration and revelation constitute the arc of inner awareness. Silence and stillness are the path to self-reflexive awareness. And the ultimate realisation is the recovery of the wholeness of the spiritual self. *Savitri* becomes *Mahakavya*, more than anything, in its attempt to recover wholeness, aesthetic and spiritual, of the complete human – and also of the author, the text and the reader. The aesthetic circle draws to a close – the akhanda rasa – in the process of complete spiritual transformation.

Notes

1. Swami Prabhavananda, *The Spiritual Heritage of India*, Mylapore: Ramakrishna Math, 1981. P 54.
2. Sri Aurobindo, *The Synthesis of Yoga* – I Book One, SABCL Vol. 20
3. http://savitrithepoem.com/about-savitri.html
4. *(See Towards an Understanding of Indian Poetry in English within Indian Critical Tradition, C. D. Narasimhaiah) https://link.springer.com/chapter/10.1007/978-1-349-27060-6_10*
5. Natyashastra 6.109, *Translated by Daniel Meyer-Dinkgräfe*
6. Generally we find all these elements in the Sanskrit Mahakavyas. (*Jarasandhavadha Mahakavyam*, PankajJani, 2010 – See Kāvyālaṅkāra of

Bhāmaha: Edited with English Translation and Notes. P.V. Naganatha Sastry. 2nd ed. Delhi: Motilal Banarsidass, 1970.

https://www.wisdomlib.org/hinduism/book/jarasandhavadha-mahakavyam/d/doc419449.html

7. For these observations from different Sanskrit acharyas, I am indebted to T Bhaskaran, *Bharatiya Kavyasastram* published by the State Institute of Languages, 1978.
8. [cf also dharma artha kama moksha, aram porul inbam veedu].
9. Nandakumar, Prema, *Dante and Sri Aurobindo*, Madras: Affiliated East-West Press, 1981, p 141.
10. See https://sreenivasaraos.com/tag/bhart%E1%B9%9Bhari/
11. See Murali,S. *The Mantra of Vision: An Overview of Sri Aurobindo's Aesthetics.* Delhi: BR, 1997.
12. See The Web of Yoga, SABCL XVII for a discussion of ananda of being) For early and late definitions of poetry– *The Sources of Poetry*, SABCL III p.105.
13. *The One Self*, Sr Aurobindo, Collected Poems, p 168

CHAPTER 5

Being and Becoming: The Premises of Sri Aurobindo's Aesthetics

> *Raso vai sah*. Bliss, verily, is the essence of existence. Taittiriya Upanishad, II.7.1

What follows is an exploration of the basic premises of Sri Aurobindo's aesthetics. Sri Aurobindo's intellectual and spiritual output is massive and his thinking quite complex to the casual reader and the uninitiated. My intent is to bring forth his continued relevance to our times. In my reading, his philosophical system – to the extent that he systematically organised it – and his poetic exploration, appear to complement each other. Whatever his major preoccupations, be it philosophy, politics or yoga, he continued to write poetry. Therefore any serious study of his aesthetics is bound to lead us toward a holistic understanding of the man his life and his thought. Because, for him, any understanding of life meant a creative understanding of reality. He pursued his spiritual quest with complete commitment and seriousness, and his *Purna Yoga* as praxis complemented his philosophical thinking toward a holistic transformation. Poetry served as an index of the evolving consciousness. This essay tries to trace his philosophical and aesthetic graphs.

Kathleen Raine, writing on *The Future Poetry*, comments on Sri Aurobindo's broad sweep and new angle of vision and observes:

> Given, therefore, his philosophic premises, and given also, his direct spiritual perceptions of the inner meaning of events whose outer aspect is alone available even to the finest not-spiritual intelligence (I think, in particular, of Rene Guenon and Coomaraswami, whose views are in this respect opposed to those of Sri Aurobindo) we must give great weight to his insight as one based on foundations that are strong, whether we regard them as philosophy or as "revealed" truth.[1]

Sri Aurobindo's pronouncements on poetry and art, she points out, might sound vague were they to come instead from any Western critic, but issuing from his mind are "precise, according to clearly understood distinctions, as between vital, mental and spiritual orders that do not exist for the Western mind,"[2] and grounded securely on strong spiritual foundations. Therefore to examine Sri Aurobindo's aesthetic theory which necessitates his definition of poetry as the Mantra of the Real,[3] and of its essential function "as a purifier and builder of the soul,"[4] to the extent of investing the ultimate aesthetic value in the divinisation of life, would require a close understanding of his spiritual insights.

Sri Aurobindo lived with his spiritual quests as we would with our everyday realities and substantially evinced much more than a severe intellectual and emotional commitment to them. "In the life of the true mystics," S. N. Dasgupta has pointed out, "beliefs exert a great formative influence. They are no mere intellectual registrations of opinions or temporary experiences, but represent the dynamic, the dominant tone of their personality as it develops and perfects itself."[5] In the case of Sri Aurobindo it was no mere belief, in the sense of a mental construct, but an intimate experiential factuality, that impelled spirituality to be the "dominant tone" of his personality. And what for a casual present-day reader, at the outset, might appear as mere metaphysical reverie or intellectual abstraction, were for him intimately felt experiences. For instance, when he writes in one of his letters referring to the first Canto of *Savitri*:

> The Inconscient and the Ignorance may be mere empty abstractions and can be dismissed as irrelevant jargon if one has not come into collision with them or plunged into their dark and bottomless reality. But to me they are realities... I was presenting a happening that was to me something sensible and, as one might say, psychologically and spiritually concrete.[6]

He reveals something more than a mere literary claim to be involved and committed to his experience; it is suggestive of a wholly integrated personality to whom the "abstract has a concreteness, substantially which is more real than the sensible form of an object or of a physical event."[7] In his various writings, that are earnest attempts to be passionately sincere to his self, Sri Aurobindo "breathed life into dogmatics."[8]

Among the chief marks of a mystic, as Coomaraswamy points out, are "a constant sense of the unity and interdependence of all life, and of the interpenetration of the spiritual and the material... So too is the sense of being everywhere at home..."[9] The Aurobindian mystique in the face of all external circumstances constantly maintained the integrity and ubiquity of the Spiritual. Writing to a disciple in 1949 about himself, Sri Aurobindo avowed:

> ...since I set foot on the Indian soil on the Apollo Bunder in Bombay, I began to have spiritual experiences, but these were not divorced from this world but had an inner infinite bearing on it, such as a feeling of the Infinite pervading material space and the Immanent inhabiting material objects and bodies. At the same time I found myself entering supraphysical worlds and planes with influences and an effect from them upon the material plane, so I could make no sharp divorce or irreconcilable opposition between what I have called the two ends of existence and all that lies between them.[10]

He goes on in this tone of experimental conviction to state his "belief": "For me all is Brahman and I find the Divine everywhere."[11] This organic, integral vision released Sri Aurobindo from the necessity of being regulated by the activities of the external world and its accepted modes. A world of psycho-spiritual reality was revealed to him, a living world, luminous and potent, dwelling in the infinitude of a Being, at once Consciousness and Bliss, which in turn was a violent denial of the neat segregation of the Material and the Spiritual. Coomaraswamy, contrasting the "inferior" with the "superior" man distinguishes the latter, in the words of Chuang Tsu, that "they live in accordance with their own nature. In the whole world they have no equal. They regulate their life by inward things."[12] The inwardness of all things, as Sri Aurobindo found, was the "Lord within them, the Divine Self and Purusha in the heart of the creature, *Isvarah sarvabhutanam hrddese*."[13] It was revealed to him that the Infinite was behind all things finite and so he sought to adjudge all values in terms of the Infinite, of which they were but imperfect translations and in which they discovered their natural consummation. The realisation of the Supreme became, for him, the most essential thing. And towards this end he organised his entire life and being. Everything else – politics, societal life and even family relationships – disintegrated in the outer circumference of this spiritual vortex. As he wrote in an article in the *Karmayogin* July 24, 1909: "The greatness of individuals is the greatness of the eternal Energy within."[14] And his lines on Aswapathy in *Savitri* would be an adequate account of himself:

> His days were a long growth to the Supreme.
> A skyward being nourishing its roots
> On sustenance from occult spiritual founts
> Climbed through white rays to meet an unseen Sun.[15]

In Sri Aurobindo's asseveration of the primary of the Spirit, one could read not only a declaration of the personal necessity for his inner growth, but also an affirmation of the spiritual consciousness of a race swept off its balance by the bedeviled forces of a materialist secular consciousness. As his insight was to confirm later, a materialist culture was socially necessitated to carefully ward off the superior integral powers of the Spiritual. He wrote in *The Synthesis of Yoga*:

> The whole aim of material man is to live to pass from birth to death with as much comfort or enjoyment as may be on the way, but any how to live... Self, domesticity, the accustomed order of the society and of the nation are the constituents of the material existence... But to the man who would assert for himself the liberty of spiritual experience and the spiritual life, he assigns, if he admits him at all, not the vestment of the priest but the robe of the Sannyasin. Outside society let him exercise his dangerous freedom. So he may even serve as a human lightning-rod receiving the electricity of the Spirit and turning it away from the social edifice.[16]

Thus Sri Aurobindo's spirituality should be seen in a global perspective; it was as much part of his social and political consciousness as it was of his religious, This ceaseless endeavour to view life in its totality signifies the most outstanding fact about his spiritual standpoint. Right from his earliest contact with the Indian situation which came only as a second phase after his European exposure Sri Aurobindo was convinced of the legitimacy of an integral awareness. And what he came to identify as the two negations – the materialist's denial of an eternal Being behind the phenomenal and the ascetic's refusal to accept the reality of the world – were as he saw it the two major impediments in the way towards a comprehensive awareness and affirmation in the history of human thought, and a new and rich self-fulfilment in an integral existence for the individual and the race alike. In his words:

> In Europe and in India, respectively, the negation of the materialist and the refusal of the ascetic have sought to assert themselves as the sole truth and to dominate the conception of Life. In India, if the result has been a great heaping up of the treasures of the Spirit, – or of some of them, -it has also been a great bankruptcy of Life; in Europe, the fullness of riches and the triumphant mastery of this world's powers and possessions have progressed towards an equal bankruptcy in the things of the Spirit.[17]

He sought to integrate life and spirit into a cosmic whole and to embody the unified vision in an ascent to Gnostic humanity. This call towards an integralist attitude might also be traced to the apparently contradictory nature of his historical situation. Born in India and brought up in England, the prophet of militant nationalism and the silent recluse of Pondicherry, the Yogi of the ancient Vedic temperament and the author of a prodigious variety of writings in the English language ranging from songs and sonnets to narratives and epics, from political pamphlets to philosophical treatises, he combined in himself both the West and the East. To understand his philosophy and thereby appraise his aesthetic theories which are organically unified with his philosophical insight, we have to take into account the impact of both the West and the East-the "Indian impact" because Sri Aurobindo deliberately *chose* to be an Indian.

Sri Aurobindo was born on 15th August, 1872, in Calcutta, as Aurobindo Ackroyd Ghose, the third son of Krishnadhan Ghose and Swarnalata Devi. It was a time when hundreds of years of stupor and languor permeated by inner conflicts and turbulations in the Indian scene had resulted in the consolidation of British colonialism, and concurrent to it, a new upsurge of national ethos was in the process of crystallising. But he confronted the question of what it meant to be an Indian only much later, when he returned from England, a fiery young man of twenty-one, seasoned in European classical learning, well-versed in Greek and Latin, and eminently ratiocinative. His early writings in the *Bandemataram* and the *Karmayogin* about India and her heritage were more of a justification for his national identity of which he was only slowly becoming aware, and a violent reaction against the colonised experience. But later, as his politics took him deeper and deeper into the very heart of nationalism, and his reading revealed to him the essence of Indian wisdom, he, despite the inner pressure in him to identify with what was a partisan view, chose an integral cosmic stance. This is what makes Sri Aurobindo, as Mokashi Punekar has said, "a unique phenomenon." For, "He is not a mere product of the Hindu resurgence, he brought to it a creative continuity with European thought."[18]

Everything that he wrote argues not merely for the integral conservation of higher values of existence, but also for a progressive increase of the levels of being, and the increasing progression calls for a new heaven and a new earth. Similarly there is evidenced a radical difference in his later mature writings as they are naturally the products of a qualitatively higher order than the earlier work. However, there does endure a discernible design for a massive visionary and critical structure in Sri Aurobindo's earlier writings to be constantly and periodically modified and developed later. He was never a systematic philosopher though. His writings bear testimony but to his deep-felt inner experiences. They embody the essentially poetic vision of a Rishi, seer-poet. His aesthetics is inherently implied in the creative experience of reality and not an aesthetic theory that is inferred intellectually and systematically. Hardly can it be said of any other poet or philosopher as can be said of him that they lived their poetic visions.

In sheer bulk and variety of subjects his creative output is stupendous: apart from translations from Sanskrit, Greek and other languages, social and political writings, philosophical treatises, speculations on the Veda, Upanishad and the Gita and massive volumes on Yoga, his work includes two epics and some two hundred odd poems. He undertook all this without any appeal for public recognition, literary acceptance or social status. A quiet man with a serious disposition and an intense passion for literature and thought, Sri Aurobindo was, as Romain Rolland chose to describe him, "the most noble representative of the Neo-Vedantic spirit… the foremost of Indian thinkers," and also, "the completest synthesis that has been realised to this day of the genius of Asia and the genius of Europe," and the last of the great Rishis who held in his hand "in firm and unrelaxed grip, the bow of creative energy."[19] Anyone who came into the circle of this creative personality experienced a strange mystic rapture, the extreme form of which Dilip Kumar Roy notes:

> I can only say that in his presence I felt myself gripped by a silent wonder and intense longing to lay my utter self at his feet and lie cradled in his indefinable Grace.[20]

Variously compared with Hegel, Bergson, Bradley and Heidegger and classed with Radhakrishnan as a notable philosopher, with Gandhi and Tagore as a leader of modern India, and ranked with Sri Ramakrishna and Maharshi Ramana as a saint, Sri Aurobindo's life falls into three distinct phases. At the age of seven he was taken to England and with his coming back to India in 1893 the first European phase ends and the political one begins. Seventeen years of militant nationalistic activities landed him in jail where the most significant experience of his life occurred – a mystic vision of Krishna-which brought in an entirely new dimension to his life and work. Although this event marks a turning point in his life and the beginning of its third phase, the earlier experiences were but preparatory to this. The developing life of a true mystic traces a gradual ascent in the scale of experience and values; Sri Aurobindo's life is rich and complete in its many-sided development and follows a clear pattern of ascent and integration. From the Cambridge scholar through the militant patriot to the silent Yogi of Pondicherry it delineates a qualitative transformation, integrating everything which has gone before into a higher plane of consciousness.[21] William James wrote: "The life of the saints are a history of successive renunciations of complication, one form of contact with the outer life being dropped after another, to save the purity of the inner tone."[22] An analysis of Sri Aurobindo's public experiences, his "exterior life," would arrive at the same conclusion as is reached by him existentially in the most private of his interior self, and poetically expressed.

> As so he grew into his larger self,
> Humanity framed his movements less and less;
> A greater being saw a greater world.[23]

With Sri Aurobindo the conventional division of the outer and inner world, subjective and objective reality, is no longer meaningful. To him action was the essence of life but it did not mean a turbulent agitation on the physical plane; it was an action that came by a conscious subjection and merging of the ego in the divine Self, a liberating action. "When we strive to act, the forces of nature do their will with us," Sri Aurobindo explains in an early article, "when we grow still, we become their master… The more complete the calm… the greater the force in action."[24] To the man whose intellect is delivered from the enslavement to dualities, from the oppositions of inner and outer, silence is the superior action – the accent is on "being" rather than "doing." Thus the "action" of the "superior man" often stands apart in a clear variance from the ordinary.

> When he acts, men will call him *unmatta*, a mad man, eccentric or idiot; for his actions will often seem to have no definite result or purpose, to be wild, unregulated, regardless of sense and probability or inspired by a purpose, a vision which is not for this world. And it is true that he follows a light which other men do not possess or would even call darkness; that what is a dream to them, is to him a reality; that their night is his day. And this is the root of the difference that, while they reason, he knows.[25]

And as a man who "knew." Sri Aurobindo left politics as suddenly and unceremoniously as he had come in. For a writer in whom the man and the work are necessarily one, this transformation from the militant political activist to the self-exiled recluse calls for closer attention.

Sri Aurobindo passed thirteen years, from 1893 to 1906, at Baroda working in various government departments and later teaching French and English in the Baroda College. These were years of self-culture, literary activity and secret political engagements. He studied Sanskrit and other Indian languages, assimilated the spirit of Indian culture and civilisation, and in 1904 began practicing Yoga, starting with *pranayama* as explained to him by a friend, a disciple of Brahmananda.[26] There was, as he found, no conflict or wavering between Yoga and politics – when he started Yoga he carried on both without any idea of opposition between them. In 1908 he met Vishnu Bhaskar Lele of Gwalior, who advanced him further in Yoga giving him a greater insight, strength and faith, and more confidence in himself. By this time he had left Baroda and taken up the position of the Principal of the newly founded Bengal National College in Calcutta. Then on till 1907 when he was arrested for sedition and later acquitted, he wrote and spoke for a new national awareness, preached a militant activism and meditated on God and man. The *Bandemataram*, the newspaper and weekly that he jointly edited with Bepin Chandra Pal, carries the bulk of his early political pamphleteering prior to being prosecuted; the *Karmayogin* and the *Dharma*, in English and in Bengali repectively, which he edited single-handedly, following his acquittal, sound a markedly different tone from these early rebellious incitements – they reveal the workings of a mind and an inner spiritual energy pressing upon it for an exclusive concentration. In a speech delivered at Uttarpara on May 30, 1909, published in the *Karmayogin*, he gave utterance to his remarkable spiritual experiences in the Alipore jail. As the walls of materiality crumbled around him revealing the omnipresence of Krishna, Sri Aurobindo underwent an experiential conviction of all that he had earlier gathered intellectually from his readings of the Gita, the Upanishads and the Vedas.

> I looked at the jail that secluded me from men and it was no longer by its high walls that I was imprisoned; no, it was Vasudeva who surrounded me. I walked under the branches of the tree in front of my cell but it was not the tree, I knew it was Vasudeva, it was Sri Krishna whom I saw standing there and holding over me his shade. I looked at the bars of my cell, the very grating that did duty for a door and again I saw Vasudeva. It was Narayana who was guarding and standing sentry over me.[27]

This experience convinced him of the fact that all beings are united in One Self, but divided by a certain separateness of consciousness, an ignorance of their true self. He found that it was possible through certain psychological disciplines to remove this veil of separating consciousness and become aware of the true Being, the Divinity within and without. In Yoga, Sri Aurobindo found a means of inward living and transformation.

The distinctive character of all saintliness is a voluntary and complete surrender to a supreme power: Sri Aurobindo obeyed an *adesa*, a command from within, and left politics for ever and withdrew into the silence of Pondicherry, there to practice and perfect his Integral Yoga. For the remaining forty years of his life, he "preached and lived the freedom of man, the unity of mankind, and the divinity of man."[28]

In Sri Aurobindo's vision the theoretical is bound up with the practical – gnosis and praxis – the metaphysical is integrated with the psychological. His philosophy is not an abstract theoretical system but a concise register of his experiences, and his finding that certain mantras of the Rig Veda substantially corroborated his own experiences strengthened his conviction of their validity.[29]

In the Vedic hymns, Sri Aurobindo discovered a considerable body of profound psychological thought and experience lying neglected, too often grossly misread. As he notes in *The Secret of the Veda* (p.34), like the majority of educated Indians he too had passively accepted without any personal verification the conclusions of European scholarship both as to the religious and as to the historical and ethnical sense of the ancient Vedic hymns. A close-reading, enriched and illumined in turn by his own inner experiences convinced him that the Vedas are the creation of an intuitive age anterior to our intellectual philosophies and not the mere ritualistic doctrines of a primitive religion. "From the historical point of view, "he wrote, "the Rig-Veda may be regarded as a record of a great advance made by humanity by special means at a certain period of its collective progress" (pp. 8-9). It is the spirit's hymn of battle and victory as it discovers and climbs to planes of thought and experience inaccessible to the natural or "mental man," man's praise of the Divine at work in the mortal. The Rishi was not the individual composer of the hymn, but the seer, *drsta*, of an eternal truth and supra-personal knowledge. He was the seeker of a higher than mental knowledge, relying entirely upon intuition and spiritual experience and manipulated the word as suggestion for the illumination toward which he was striving. And the very act of composing the hymn was to him,

> a means of spiritual progress for himself and for others. It rose out of his soul, it became a power of his mind, it was the vehicle of his self-expression in some important or even critical moment of his life's inner history. (pp. 9-10)

This essential poetic vision of the Rig-Veda accorded Sri Aurobindo the basic pattern for an integrated view of all and everything, a harmonious truth of being, a spiritual completeness, and the foundations for his philosophy of the Divine life. *Ekam sad vipra bahudha vadanti*, says the Rig Veda (1.164.46) – the Existent is One, the sages express it variously. But it was the Vedic idea of the inner life of man that Sri Aurobindo saw as the central point of its importance. Convinced of the double function of the Vedic imagery – at once exoteric and esoteric – his psychological reading of the verses re-revealed their complex symbolism: the ascending graded scale of the Vedic worlds corresponded to a similar mounting scale of planes or degrees of consciousness in the nature of man, that is, man subjectively contained in himself all the worlds that objectively contained him. Through their hieratic hymns the Rishis were, he found, denoting the transition of the human soul from a state of death to a state of immortality, from a divided, and limited being to an integral and infinite being.

> Death is the mortal state of Matter with Mind and Life involved in it; Immorality is a state of infinite being, consciousness and bliss. Man rises beyond the two firmaments *rodasi*, Heaven and Earth, mind and body, to the infinity of the Truth, Mahas, and so to the divine Bliss. This is the "great passage" discovered by the Ancestors, the anciet Rishis. (p. 43)

Taking his cue from the symbolism of the worlds in the Vedic conception of the *Vyahrtis*, the three symbolic words of the mantra, *Om bhur bhuvah svah*, and the three cosmic divisions of *prthivi, antariksa* and *dyau*, completed correspondingly by the Puranic and Vedantic worlds, Sri Aurobindo posited the ascending gradations of Matter, Life and Mind, and the three higher worlds of Sat-chit-ananda as constituting the entire range of being. And between the lower hemisphere or *aparardha* of Matter, Life and Mind, and the higher hemisphere or *parardha*, of Sat-chit-ananda he envisioned the plane of the Supermind which corresponded to the Vedic world of *satyam rtam brhat* and the fourth Vyahrti of the Upanishad-Mahas. This Supermind is the divine Creatrix, in the Aurobindian vision, through which the Supreme Spirit involutes itself in the phenomenal being. And the entire meaning of existence is grounded in the progressive revelation of this *involuted* spirit. As he sets it out in *The Life Divine*:

> The Divine descends from pure existence through the play of Consciousness – Force and Bliss and the creative medium of Supermind into cosmic being; we ascend from Matter through a developing life, soul and mind and the illuminating medium of Supermind towards the divine being. The knot of the two, the higher and the lower hemisphere, is where mind and Supermind meet with a veil between them. The rending of the veil is the condition of the divine life in humanity… (p. 264)

The conquest of Truth out of the darkness of Ignorance, and consequently the conquest of Immortality, which was the central conception of the Veda, authentically vindicated his belief that the ascent to the divine Life is the human journey (p. 42).

Sri Aurobindo pursued this Vedic idea further and evolved his notion of the ultimate spiritualisation of Matter, Life and Mind by a revelation and effectuation of the involuted Spirit. On the strength of his personal experience, he was assured that Consciousness was the essential principle of the whole universe and all existence was a slow evolutionary unfolding. The *Mundaka Upanishad* substantiates this view: *tapasa ciyate brahma* (1.1.8), by contemplative power Brahman expands. Matter is nothing but Brahmin-energized-Consciousness. It is not customary in Western philosophy to distinguish between "mental" and "conscious," but this distinction is vital to Sri Aurobindo's thought. As he explains in a letter:

> Consciousness is usually identified with mind, but mental consciousness is only the human range which no more exhausts all the possible ranges of consciousness than human sight exhausts all the gradations of colour or human hearing all the gradation of sound – for there is much above or below that is to man invisible and inaudible. So there are ranges of consciousness above and below the human range, with which the normal human has no contact and they seem to it unconscious, -supramental or overmental and submental ranges… The Brahman state is that of a supreme existence supremely aware of itself, *svayamprakasa*, – it is Sachchidananda, Existence-Consciousness-Bliss.[30]

Although consciousness is one integral whole, there were different statuses, *avastha*, of it, existential grades or levels ranging from the Spirit which is Absolute Consciousness to the apparently unconscious Matter which is nothing but dormant consciousness, the Inconscient, and "involved state of consciousness which like the Tao or Shunya, though in a different way, contains all things suppressed within it so that under a pressure from above or within all can evolve out of it…"[31]

The phenomenal world is but an extension of Being, a part of the Spirit's self-expression, and thus enfolds a divine possibility, and as Sri Aurobindo sees it, that possibility is evolutionary. Man himself is a doubly involved being- most of his self in mind and below is involved in a subliminal consciousness and most of his self above mind is involved in a spiritual consciousness. In the Aurobindian vision the present mental consciousness is not the last word in the evolutionary unfolding of Being, which is the divine Lila, but only one stage in the cosmic subway. The Supermind is the next evolutionary possibility. It is a plane of unified consciousness which wholly preserves a self-awareness by identity in a totality of extension of all Being, in its surface finite appearance as well as in its intrinsic infiniteness. The transition from mind to Supermind could be effected only by a radical shift in consciousness. And his perfecting of an Integral Yoga was a dynamic attempt towards an integration and harmonisation of mind and Supermind, nature and *supernature.*

Although he had started the practice of Yoga as far back as 1904, it was only in the isolation of Pondicherry that he could devote his entire being to the pursuit of this higher life uniting and harmonising the two ends of existence, Matter and Spirit. In his exploration of the occult planes of being he was aided and seconded by his Yogic coadjutor Mirra Richard, later the "Mother," whose experiences in this regard, as he himself warranted, dovetailed with his. It was her husband, Paul Richard, who collaborated with him in the launching of the philosophical journal *Arya* in which all the major works of Sri Aurobindo – *The Life Divine, The Synthesis of Yoga, The Secret of the Veda, Essays on the Gita, The Future Poetry, The Human Cycle, The Foundations of Indian Culture* and others-were serialised. Sri Aurobindo's vision, as it emerges from his works, is nothing if not "global," He does not attempt to consciously construct any system, instead "there is a harmonising of the different parts of a many-sided knowledge so that all unites logically together."[32] And it is not enforced by any logical argument but "by a clear vision of the relations and sequences of Knowledge."[33] A fuller idea of life demands of man that he find an integral living founded upon an eternal Truth, a metaphysic that recognises a divine Reality substantial to the world of matter, life and mind-the *philosophia perennis*,[34] and such a view is implied in the heart of every one of the higher religions. The philosophical position of Sri Aurobindo is not different from this, and through his Yoga he attempted a conscious union of the self with the Self. By the term Yoga, he means:

> a methodised effort towards self-perfection by the expression of the potentialities latent in the being and a union of the human individual with the universal and transcendent Existence we see partially expressed in man and in the Cosmos.[35]

In the Aurobindian sense all life is either consciously or subconsciously a Yoga. In *The Synthesis of Yoga* he declares emphatically: "All life is Yoga," (p. 4) Behind the phenomenal world of appearances he perceived the vast Yoga of nature attempting to unite with the essential Divine, and this cosmic unfolding has arrived at mental man through a releasing of the involuted life from matter and mind from life. The "mental being" that man is, he has been endowed with self-conscious means and will-power to expedite the ever-increasing expression of nature's potentialities

> Spirit is the crown of universal existence; Matter is its basis; Mind is the link between the two. Spirit is that which is eternal; Mind and Matter are its workings. Spirit is that which is concealed and has to be revealed; mind and body are the means by which it seeks to reveal itself. Spirit is the image of the Lord of the Yoga; mind and body are the means He has provided for reproducing that image in phenomenal existence. All nature is an attempt at a progressive revelation of the concealed Truth, a more and more successful reproduction of the divine image. (p. 24)

Yoga effects a rapid revolution in what is a slow evolution in nature. As Vivekananda pointed out, Yoga may be regarded as a means of compressing one's evolution into a single life or a few years or even a few months of bodily existence (p. 2).

In this monumental treatise, *The Synthesis of Yoga*, Sri Aurobindo explores the possibilities of the varieties of Yoga prevalent in India, and formulates an Integral Yoga – a syncretic essence of its ancient prototypes. Sri Aurobindo's vision went beyond what was previously achieved by the disciplines of Jnana, Hatha, Bhakti and Tantric Yoga systems, and his intention being to achieve what had not been hitherto achieved, he was necessitated to break new grounds. Because it aimed not at an escape into a Nirvana but at a total change of life and existence, a supra-cosmic achievement, he felt that his Yoga was "not a retreading of old walks, but a spiritual adventure."[36] This integral way to the Truth invoked certain psychological disciplines leading to an inner spiritual transformation, a widening of consciousness out of the confines of the ego and the body, an opening up to the higher Divine Consciousness and a bringing down, or the descent of the Supramental Divine with a consequent transformation of mind, life and body. Sri Aurobindo repeatedly insisted on the perfecting of the material body and its "divinisation" as the ultimate triumph of the Spirit.

In *The Life Divine*,[37] he calls attention to the discovery of the ancient occult sciences that the body is not the whole *even* of our physical being; its gross density is not all of our substance. The Oldest Vedantic knowledge tells us of five degrees of our being – the material, the vital, the mental, the ideal, the spiritual, and to each of these grades of our soul there corresponds a grade of our substance, a sheath as it was called in the ancient figurative language. A later psychology found that these five sheaths of our substance were the material of three bodies – gross-physical, subtle and causal – in all of which the soul simultaneously dwells, although we are presently conscious only of the material. The Tantric psychology discovered six vibratory nodules or centres *(chakra)* in the material body corresponding to six centres of life and mind faculties in the subtle plane, and one higher centre above the head. With Yoga these centres open releasing their energy and flooding the entire being.[38] In the order of the ascending force of the *Kundalini sakti*, or the coiled and sleeping serpent power within, the centres are; *muladhara cakra* which governs the physical down to the subconscient, *svadhisthana cakra* which governs the lower vital, *nabhipadma* or *manipura chakra* which governs the larger vital, *hrtpadma* or *anahata cakra* which governs the emotional being, *visuddha cakra* which governs the expressive and externalising mind, *ajnacakra* which governs the dynamic mind, will, vision, mental formation, and *sahasradala cakra* the above centre which governs the higher mental regions that Sri Aurobindo terms the *Higher Mind*, the *Illumined Mind*, opening to the *Intuition*, the *Overmind* and above it the *Supermind* itself.

Sri Aurobindo's Yoga incorporating these Tantric planes and energy centres, differs from the traditional in the opening order of the Chakras.[39] In the Tantric system they open from down upwards, beginning with the *muladhara*; in the Integral Yoga the descending supramental force opens these centres from top to bottom. The bursting open of these centres would install a Yogic consciousness in the place of the ordinary. Writing on Sri Aurobindo's Yoga and exemplifying it with his own unique inner experiences, Satprem comments:

> Once in possession of these centres, the seeker begins to know beings, things, the world and himself in their reality, as they are, for he no longer catches external signs, no longer doubtful words, gestures, all that immured dumb show, nor the veiled face of things, but the pure vibration in each thing, each being, at every stage, which nothing can camouflage.[40]

Thus through his Yoga it is a spiritualisation of consciousness that Sri Aurobindo proposes. In his vision "Supramental" or divine forces above the *sahasradala* use it for their transit and thus spiritualise the entire being. What the whole process demands is a single-mindedness of purpose and will. "He who seeks the Divine must consecrate himself to God and to God only."[41]

When he writes of his Yoga that it is "an ecstatic contemplation; it seeks not to pass into the being of the Divine, but to bring the Divine into ourselves and to lose ourselves in the deep ecstasy of his presence or of his possession; and its bliss is not the peace of unity, but the ecstasy of union,"[42] it is the intense yearning of the soul for the Divine in the more intimate Yoga of Bhakti or Adoration that we detect. It is significant in this context that Sri Aurobindo writing on the Gita attributes the highest value to the Bhakti Yoga while relegating all other Yogas including Jnana to the secondary status. He notes:

> This knowledge [Integral Knowledge] comes, says the Gita, by a highest Bhakti. It is attained when the mind exceeds itself by a supramental and high spiritual seeing of things and when the heart too rises in unison beyond our more ignorant mental forms of love and devotion to a love that is calm and deep and luminous with widest knowledge, to a supreme delight in God and an illimitable adoration, the unperturbed ecstasy, the spiritual Ananda.[43]

Here and elsewhere when he speaks of Yoga as ecstatic devotion and surrender, and speaks of the world as the play of the Divine, and exulting in a passionate bliss of identity writes, "Thy spirit's infinite breath I feel in me;/ My life is a throb of Thy eternity,"[44] it is reflective of a more profound and significant extension of the spirit of Vaishnava Bhakti – a sensuous experience of the Spiritual.

The Aurobindian aesthetics, as has been pointed out, is an aesthetics inherent or implied in the creative experience of reality. As he experientially realised, the essence of all thing is the infinite Divine truth of being at once conscious and blissful – Sachchidananda – and to be, as he envisioned it, is to become complete in Divine Being, in consciousness of Being, in delight of Being and an integrated completeness of Being. This process begins with an inward living and culminates in an integral divine living. We read in *The Life Divine*:

> All being is one and to be fully is to be all that is, To be in the being of all and to include all in one's being, to be conscious of the consciousness of all, to be integrated in force with the universal force, to carry all action and experience in oneself and feel it as one's own action and experience, to feel all delight of being as one's own delight of being is a necessary condition of the integral divine living. (p. 1025)

It is the Soul, or the diviner element in man that is the aesthetic being in him, exulting and expanding in Consciousness by Godward experience, rising on its own curve to its divine consummation. "To find highest beauty is to find God; to reveal, to embody, to create, as we say, highest beauty is to bring out of our souls the living image and power of God."[45] The Aurobindian aesthetics is thus an aesthetics of transcendence and transformation. It is more a psychology of aesthetic experience than a philosophy of beauty that he propounds. For, embedded in his life and writings alike, is the deep-felt inner compulsion of the spiritual that endeavours to see the beauty and bliss of the Divine in life and man, and nature, and desires their just transformation in order to reveal the veiled Real.

The Yoga of Sri Aurobindo is central to his aesthetics, in fact his is a Yogic aesthetics. "A Yogi who writes is not a literary man," Sri Aurobindo explains to a disciple in one of his letters, "for he writes only what the inner Will and Word wants him to express. He is a channel and an instrument of something greater than his own literary personality."[46] Once the communion with the "Cosmic Thinker" is established ideas and utterances crowd in from within or from above for creative expression. His own experience was that, Yoga brought in its wake inspiration and new values. "Everything that I wrote," Sri Aurobindo claimed, "came from my Yogic experience, knowledge and inspiration… from the heightening of my consciousness and the greater inspiration that came from the heightening."[47] And it may not be surprising that a man in whom there is no separating the Yogic-spiritual knowledge of Divinity from the intense will to become that ultimately, should choose the poetic mode as a consummate expression, for in his vision the poetic word was the "vehicle of the spirit, the chosen medium of the soul's self-expression."[48] The highest function of poetry, in his view, as "a purifier and builder of the soul," enhanced its kinship with Yoga. However, all art which are "at once work and knowledge," and "a realisation of something of the play of the Infinite," could be made "a means of God-realisation or of divine formation" if executed in the required spirit of a religious offering and with inner purity and devotion. "The Yogin's aim in the Arts," he says, "should not be a mere aesthetic, mental or vital gratification, but, seeing the Divine everywhere, worshipping it with a revelation of the meaning of its works, to express that one Divine in gods and men and creatures and objects."[49] Art was a link between the visible and the invisible, the apparent and the Real, in so far as it opened a passage between the external consciousness and the inner mind. Sri Aurobindo's idea of the Supreme Spirit is in consonance with the traditional Indian notion of *rasovai sah*,[50] Bliss, verily, is the essence of existence, and the highest possibility of all art is to merge into the self-delight of this Infinite. Yet, the poetic art, Sri Aurobindo held dearer primarily on account of its "instrument, the rhythmic word, is fuller of subtle and immaterial elements," and secondly, being "the most complex, flexible, variously suggestive of all the instruments of the artistic creator, it has more – almost infinite – possibilities in many directions than any other." [51] It is significant that throughout his life, it was only to the order of a poet that Sri Aurobindo ever made any claim. And whatever vocations he passed through he never stopped writing poetry; over and above his relentless experiments in form and metre, the poetic act was manipulated as a means of ascension to the superconscient planes. Poetry, he says, is "a question of the right concentrated silence or seeking somewhere in the mind with the right openness to the Word that is trying to express itself…"[52] As his Yogic practices increased his creativity too underwent a consequent transformation, a gradual ascent in poetic consciousness as he entered the higher mental regions, hardly accessible to the normal poetic minds. His poetry was his ceaseless attempt towards a closer approximation to the *mantra*, the Word beyond the silence.

Although Sri Aurobindo never consciously developed any aesthetic system, from what is overly his dissertation on a personal poetics – *The Future Poetry* – and a large number of letters to various disciples particularly on topics related to aesthetics, we can safely assume that he was familiar with the span of Western critical tradition from Aristotle up to T. S. Eliot, and more particularly the English critical tradition from Ben Jonson, Sydney and Dryden to the twentieth century, and also the Indian tradition with its emphasis on *rasa* and *dhvani* in the line of law-givers like Bharata, Bhatta Nayaka, Mammata, Anandavardhana and Abhinavagupta. Being a radical visionary his preference or acceptance of any aesthetic proposition was not by mere intellectual agreement but by a deep intuitive insight which demanded harmony and integration rather than anything else. So long as the philosophical stand he had taken could claim originality apart from its pivotal Vedic foundations, the aesthetic theory that emerges from a close reading of his works, could claim equal originality, because it is an offshoot of the selfsame subjective experience – in Aurobindian terms we might call it "spiritualised aesthetic." All art, as Sri Aurobindo sees it, in its own way, seeks to arrive at a concentrated expression of the Spirit, and it is from the "Soul" that the expression originates and it is to the soul that it unveils the Real. As mentioned earlier, the soul, in Aurobindian terminology, is the aesthetic being. It is the *antaratman*, the inner self, the true creator and recipient of the aesthetic delight or *ananda* which in the language of Indian spirituality, is the essential delight the Infinite feels in itself and in its creation. In the words of Sri Aurobindo:

> The world is a movement of God in His own being; we are the centres and knots of divine consciousness which sum up and support the processes of His movement. The world is His play with His own self-conscious delight, He who alone exists, infinite, free and perfect; we are the self-multiplications of that conscious delight, thrown out into being to be His playmates. The world is a formula, a rhythm, a symbol-system expressing God to Himself in His own consciousness, -it has no material existence but exists only in His consciousness and self-expression; we, like God, are in our inward being That which is expressed, but in our outward being terms of that formula, notes of that rhythm, symbols of that system. Let us lead forward God's movement, play out His play, work out His formula, execute His harmony, express Him through ourselves in His system. This is our joy and our self-fulfilment; to this end we who transcend and exceed the universe, have entered into universe-existence.[53]

And herein lies Sri Aurobindo's principle of delight and *ananda* which is cardinal to his aesthetics. This Ananda is part of the eternal ontological order, and is in the direct line of the *rasa* theory of art which is central to the Indian aesthetics tradition and postulates Rasa as designating the totality of the aesthetic experience – the creative experience of the artist, the aesthetic relish by the *sahrdaya*, the experiencer of like-heart with the artist, and the essence of the created real, all identical in an inalienable delight and bliss. But in Sri Aurobindo's aesthetics, as with everything else in his system, there is no finality to the evolving aesthetic boundary. The soul of man, like all phenomenal being, is in constant endeavour to evolve from its unfinished nature and get into a unity with the Spirit through its multiform manifestation and on many different planes. It is a constant becoming. According to Sri Aurobindo, in art this endeavour reveals itself in a sort of evolution from the objective to the inward and from the inward to the inmost, the spiritual – a constant labour of self-enlargement. Applying this characteristic insight to the history of art and poetry down the ages, he has shown in *The Future Poetry*, the evolutionary development of the aesthetic consciousness within the organism of the race. This general evolution has its own natural periods or ages, but it is not necessarily linear or sequential; very often there are reversals, anticipations and returns. Every nation, Sri Aurobindo found, has or develops a spirit in its inner being a special soul-form and a law of its nature which determines the course of its evolution. All its self-expression would be conditioned by this soul-form. And it is the English spirit, the meeting place of the Teuton and the Celt, which reveals itself to the seer's vision as the excellent instance of a national creative spirit describing with remarkable fidelity the natural curve and stages of the psychological evolution of poetry. That Sri Aurobindo chose to devote a major portion of his hieratic *ars poetica*, *The Future Poetry,* to trace the evolution of English poetry from Chaucer to the twentieth century, goes to prove the burden of importance he places on that poetry. Towards the end of his book, he qualifies his choice:

> It is a literature that has long done great things but has never exhausted its great natural vigor nor fixed itself in any dominant tradition, but rather has constantly shown a free spirit of poetical adventure and a perfect readiness to depart from old moorings and set its sail to undiscovered countries. It has an unsurpassed power of imaginative and intuitive language and has shown it to a very high degree in the intuitive expression of the life soul and to some degree in that of the inspired intelligence. It seems therefore a predestined instrument for a new poetic language of the intuitive spirit. (p. 271)

Despite the fact that English poetry is more powerfully and consciously personal and individual than any other, and aims much less directly at the impersonal and universal (p. 53), Sri Aurobindo discerns the ascending curve of the human spirit in its imaginative self-expression.

The earliest motive and style of the English creative spirit as it emerges in Chaucer and strikes a distinct English note, is a direct and concrete poetic observation of ordinary human life and character. As Sri Aurobindo notes,

> Chaucer has his eye fixed on the object, and that object is the visible action of life as it passes before him throwing its figures on his mind and stirring it to a kindly satisfaction in the movement and its interest... He is not concerned to look at all into the souls or deeply into the minds of the men whose appearance, action and easily apparent traits of character he describes with so apt and observant a fidelity. (p. 59)

The objective developed into a vital poetry of the Elizabethans, "a poetry of the power and beauty and wonder and spontaneous though, the joy and passion and pain" (p. 57), where the externals of life were heightened by a vital dynamism. This great period of dramatic poetry with its Marlowe who "knows that the human soul in action is his subject and Karma the power of the theme," (p. 67) and Shakespeare, who was "not primarily an artist, a poetic thinker or anything else of the kind, but a great vital creator and intensely, though within marked limits, a seer of life" (p. 69), was an expression of the vital energy of the life-spirit. With the next phase, that of the Augustans the Latin "intellectuality" is evidenced, and Milton with his "too imperfect grandiose epic... the one supreme fruit left by the attempt of English poetry to seize the classical manner, achieve beauty of poetic expression disciplined by a high intellectual severity and forge a complete balance and measured perfection of architectonic form and structure" (p. 80), Pope, Dryden and their school obsessed with "thinking in verse". (p. 83) gave utterance to an age where "passion is replaced by rhetoric, the heart is silent, life has civilised, urbanised, socialised and stylised itself too much to have any more a very living contact with Nature" (p. 86). Then came an attempt to exceed the intellect in the sudden emergence" of some half-mystical Celtic turn of the national mind into supra-intellectual sources of inspiration". (p. 89), in the poetry of Blake, Wordsworth, Coleridge and the other Romantics. Yet this new "dawn" in English poetry, as Sri Aurobindo chose to describe it, was, he feels, insufficiently supported by any adequate spiritual knowledge.

> This attempt did not come to perfect fusion; it stopped short partly because there had not been the right intellectual preparation or a sufficient basis of spiritual knowledge and experience; only so much could be given as the solitary individual intuition of the poet could attain by a difficult groping or a sudden sovereign effort. (p. 57)

Moreover, he reasons, the attempt failed because after the lapse into an age of reason the spontaneous or the intense language of spiritual poetry could not easily be found, or even if found could not be maintained. So we get a deviation into another age of intellectualism but one aesthetically refined and open to higher poetic summits. And partly out of this intellectuality and partly by a dissatisfaction and recoil from its limitations, has issued forth, what was then contemporary English poetry for Sri Aurobindo. It appeared to him to be

> Approaching on some of its lines and in spite of many mistakes and divagations the secret of the utterance of profounder truth and the right magic of a speech and rhythm which will be the apt body and motion of its spirit. (p. 58)

Thus for Sri Aurobindo writing in 1920, the characteristic motive of the poetry of his times was a harmonious ascension of the human intelligence to large and profound truths of the Spirit. With his greater foresight and insight, he singles out Whitman, Carpenter, Yeats, A. E. Meredith and Tagore as the harbingers of this new voice in poetry, an experimental straining after a new power of rhythm and a striving towards a more powerful expression of spiritual revelation. The temper of the change that is ushered in, he felt, is one in which

> The intellectual way of looking at things is being gradually transcended or is raising itself to a power beyond itself; it is moving through the observing mind and reflective reason towards an intimate self-experience, from thought to vision, from intellectual experiment to intuitive experience...... The whole view and sense of existence has deepened into a greater subjectivity. (p. 170)[54]

The law of progressively becoming conscious of himself is one of the fundamental laws of human existence, and poetry too reflects this trail faithfully.[55] Extended a little beyond its specificity, this evolutionary curve of English poetry can be applied to a new reading of world poetry with Homer and Chaucer representing the physical mind of the race, Kalidasa and Shakespeare the vibrant vital mind, and Vyasa, Sophocles, Virgil and Dante the intellectual mind in the rhythmic voyage of self-discovery of the human spirit. Concluding his historical survey, Sri Aurobindo observes:

> This progress of poetry... has been an index of an advance of the cultural mind of humanity which has enlarged its scope by a constant raising of the scale of the soul's experience and has now risen to a great height and breadth of intellectual vision and activity, and the question is at present of the next step in the scale of ascension, and whether it can now be firmly taken or will be missed once moew with a fall back to another retracing of the psychological circuit. (p. 238)

And as he envisions it, Spirit is the next grade above the intellect, and therefore, the intellectual of the race if at all it has to go forward, must open now to an awareness of the spiritual, "an illumined self-knowledge and God-knowledge and a world-knowledge too which transmuted in the great light will spiritualise the whole view and motive of our existence." (p. 239)

Sri Aurobindo's survey of the growth and development of English poetry as it traces the graph of evolving human awareness, is notable both for its originality of perception and for its wealth of detail – it is the aesthetic vision of a Yogi who through his catholic vision and spiritual amplitude has abundantly borne out his claim that a Yogi can accomplish any task.[56] It was revealed to him that poetic creativity progressively reforms with the higher planes of reality embraces by the poet's consciousness; the intenser and deeper his awareness, the greater and diviner the power that manifests in him. Since a fuller realisation of the potentials intrinsic to the human condition, a realising of the godhead in the world and man, is a prerogative of the Rishi or the Seer, it is to that elevated role that the poet in his passionate pursuit of the real aspires to be. And indeed, with Sri Aurobindo the idea of the poet who is a Rishi has reappeared after the Vedic times.

When Rilke declared that the task of the poet in the post-war world would be "to prepare in men's hearts the way for the gentle, mysterious, trembling transformations, from which alone the understandings and harmonies of a serener future will proceed,"[57] and Whitman spoke of the revelation and outpouring of "Godlike suggestions pressing for birth in the soul,"[58] and Rimbaud visualised the poet as being the instrument of a total transformation of humanity, a seer and a prophet,[59] we hear the reverberations of the Aurobindian oracle. When Baudelaire wrote:

> The unquenchable thirst for everything that is beyond and everything that life reveals, is the most living proof of our immortality. It is at once through poetry and across poetry… that the soul catches a glimpse of the splendours situated beyond the tomb…[60]

and more recently martin Heidegger writing on Holderlin speculated about the possibility of poetry to mediate knowledge of being and observed that "poetry is the establishing of being by means of the word,"[61] we begin to appreciate Sri Aurobindo's prophetic insight.

Erich Neumann in his Art and the Creative Unconscious writes:

> Our conception of man is beginning to change. Up to now we saw him chiefly in a historical or horizontal perspective, embedded in his group, his

> time, and his cultural canon, and determined by his position in the world – that is, in his particular epoch. There is truth in this vision, no doubt, but today we are beginning to see man in a new perspective – vertically – in his relation to the absolute.[62]

The Aurobindian poetic self experientially found Man in the Absolute; the seer-vision perceived the heart of reality. C. Day Lewis[63] points out that it is the inherent nature of the poetic vision to "perceive those invisible truths which are like electrons the basis of reality," and the nature of the poetic imagination "to become aware of the cryptic links that bind out universe together, to find similarity in difference and to make coherence out of contradiction." He goes on to assert, "If the poet is not a clairvoyant, he is nothing. And this clairvoyancy is particularly directed towards discovering the 'supernatural' in nature and the 'superhuman' in humanity." But Lewis warns us in a poem:

> Those Himalayas of the mind
> Are not so easily possessed:
> There is more than precipice and storm
> Between you and your Everest.[64]

That Sri Aurobindo, seer-poet, constantly strove towards a clarified vision of reality is quite indubitable because he combined in himself the "thinker" bhasyakar, and the poet, Kavi, and was wholly more than committed to his experience – his life experiences suggest a total integrated personality whose intellect is coterminous with his Yogic faculties. He explored in first hand terms what it meant to be a Rishi and embody in one's self the direct vision of truth *drsti*, the light in the soul. He not only desired to possess "those Himalayas of the mind," but endeavoured to transform every facet of earthly existence. And it is towards this end that he canalised his art and life, envisioning a spiritual value behind and beyond everything, a value cognised as a luminous revelation – the pleasure of being and the ecstasy of becoming.

Notes and References

1. Kathleen Raine, "The Future Poetry," *Sri Aurobindo Circle*, 15 (1959), p. 35.
2. Ibid., p. 31.
3. Sri Aurobindo, *The Future Poetry,* 2nd ed. (Pondicherry: Sri Aurobindo Ashram, 1985), p. 10. All references are to this edition.
4. Ibid., p. 208.
5. S.N. Dasgupta, *Hindu Mysticism* (Bombay: Allied, n. d.), p. ix.

6. "Sri Aurobindo's Letters on *Savitri*," included in Vol. XXIX of the *Sri Aurobindo Birth Centenary Library*, pp. 734-35. The *Sri Aurobindo Birth Centenary Library* (hereafter referred to as SABCL), published by the Sri Aurobindo Ashram, Pondicherry, 1972, in thirty volumes, incorporates the complete works of Sri Aurobindo.
7. Ibid., p. 736.
8. S. K. Nandi, *Studies in Modern Indian Aesthetics* (Simla: Indian Institute of Advanced Study, 1975), p. 156.
9. Ananda Coomaraswamy, "Cosmopolitan View of Nietzsche, "*The Dance of Shiva* (New Delhi: Sagar, 1982), p. 145.
10. *Sri Aurobindo on Himself*, SABCL XXVI, p. 98.
11. Ibid.
12. *The Dance of Shiva*, op.cit., p. 150.
13. *The Synthesis of Yoga*, SABCL XXI, p. 773.
14. SABCL III, p. 356.
15. *Savitri*, SABCL XXVIII, pp. 22-23.
16. SABCL XX, pp. 17-18. Cf. Theodore Roszak, *Where the Wasteland Ends: Politics and Transcendence in Postindustrial Society* (New York: Anchor Books, 1973): "The repression of the religious sensibilities in our culture over the past few centuries has been as much as adjunct of social and economic necessity as any act of class oppression or physical exploitation; it has been as mandatory for urban-industrial development as the accumulation of capital or the inculcation of factory discipline upon the working millions."
17. *The Life Divine*, SABCL XVIII, p. 9.
18. Shankar Mokashi Punekar, "Continuum Models in Sri Aurobindo's Thought: Some Notes, "*The Banasthali Patrika*, 17 &18 (1971-72), p. 117.
19. Romain Roland, quoted in Prema Nandakumar, *A Study of "Savitri"* (Pondicherry: All India Books, 1985), pp. 4-5.
20. Dilip Kumar Roy and Indira Devi, *Piligrims of the Stars: Autobiography of Two Yogis* (Porthill, Idaho: Timeless Books, 1973), p. 194.
21. Cf. "Evolution-Psychology – The Supermind," SABCL XVII: "At each capital step of Nature's ascent there is a reversal of consciousness in the evolving spirit. As when a climber turns on a summit to which he has labored and looks down with an exalted and wider power of vision on all that was once above or on a level with him but is now below his feet, the evolutionary being not only transcends his past self, his former now exceeded status, but commands from a higher grade of self-experience and vision, with a new apprehending feeling or a new comprehending sight and effectuating power in a greater system of values, all that was once his own consciousness but is now below him and belongs to an inferior creation."
22. William James, quoted in Prema Nandakumar, *A Study of "Savitri"*, op.cit., p. 15.

23. *Savitri*, SABCL XXVIII, p. 26.
24. "The Strength of Stillness," SABCL III, pp. 366-67.
25. Ibid, p. 368.
26. SABCL XXVI, p. 20.
27. SABCL II, p. 4.
28. AB. Purani, "Sri Aurobindo: A Brief Life-Sketch," *The Integral Philosophy of Sri Aurobindo: A Commemorative Symposium*, ed. Haridas Chaudhury and Frederic Spiegelberg [London: Geroge Allen & Unwin, 1960), p. 340.
29. *The Secret of the Veda*, SABCL, X, p. 37.
30. SABCL XXII, p. 234.
31. Ibid., p. 235.
32. *Sri Aurobindo on Himself*, SABCL XXVI, p. 374.
33. Ibid.
34. The phrase was coined by Leibniz. See Aldous Huxley, *The Perennial Philosophy* (London: Fontana, 1958).
35. The Synthesis of Yoga, SABCL XX, p. 2. *The Synthesis of Yoga* forms the volumes XX and XXI of the SABCL.
36. SABCL XXII, p. 101.
37. The following argument incorporates Sri Aurobindo's observations in *The Life Divine*, pp. 259, 931, et passim. *The Life Divine* forms the volumes XVIII and XIX of the SABCL.
38. SABCL XXII, pp. 364-72. Cf. Swami Prabhavananda, *The Spiritual Heritage of India*: "The word *Kundalini* literally means the coiled up. According to the scriptures, the divine energy remains unmanifested within us, and to the yogi's eye it has a form like that of a coiled serpent. The object of spiritual practices is to awaken this sleeping power in man. There are, assert the Tantras, seven centres of consciousness, the seventh of which is located in the brain. [sic] These centres, resembling lotuses, are technically known as cakras. Through certain prescribed exercises the kundalini, or Divine Energy, rises through the centres until it reaches the seventh, and in this seventh occurs a mystic union with the Supreme Lord, who their resides. Then it is that one attains transcendental consciousness." For a detailed study of this subject see Arthur Avalon, *The Serpent Power* (Madras: Ganesh & Co., 1913). Both Rishabchand in *The Integral Yoga of Sri Aurobindo* (Pondicherry: Sri Aurobindo Memorial Fund Society, 1953) and Satprem in *Sri Aurobindo or the Adventure of Consciousness* (Pondicherry: Sri Aurobindo Ashram Trust, 1968) treat this area in a great detail.
39. SABCL XXII, p. 74.
40. Satprem, *Sri Aurobindo or the Adventure of Consciousness*, trans. Tehmi; (1968; rpt. Pondicherry: Sri Aurobindo Ashram Trust, 1982), p. 57.
41. SABCL XX, p. 64.

42. SABCL XXI, p. 549.
43. *Essays on the Gita*, SABCL, XIII, p. 518.
44. "Bliss of Identity," *Collected Poems*, SABCL V.
45. *The Human Cycle*, SABCL XV, p. 135.
46. *Sri Aurobindo on Himself*, SABCL XXVI, p. 221.
47. Ibid.
48. *The Future Poetry*, p. 255. Cf. Stephen Spender on Rilke, "Rilke views this realisation of consciousness of nature, the past, God, as the supreme task of man. The task is to make the forces outside him become conscious through him. Poetry is a means, though not the only one, by which this can be achieved. But it is supreme in being the use of language in which all transformation become imagined and explicit."
49. SABCL XX, p. 133.
50. *Taittiriya Upanishad*, II.7.1.
51. *The Future Poetry*, P. 11.
52. "Letters on Poetry, Literature and Art," SABCL IX, p. 391.
53. "The Web of Yoga," SABCL XVII, p. 50.
54. Cf. W. B. Yeats, "The Autum of the Body": "Our thoughts and emotions are often but spray flung up from hidden tides that follow a moon no eye can see. I remember that when I first began to write I desired to describe outward things as vividly as possible, and took pleasure, in which there was, perhaps, a little discontent, in picturesque and declamatory books. And then quite suddenly I lost the desire of describing outward things, and found that I took little pleasure in a book unless it was spiritual and unemphatic. I did not then understand that the change was from beyond my own mind, but I understand now that writers are struggling all over Europe, though not often with a philosophic understanding of their struggle, against that picturesque and declamatory way of writing, against that 'externality' which a time of scientific and political thought has brought into literature. This struggle has been going on for some years, but it has only just become strong enough to draw within itself the little inner world which alone seeks more than amusement in the arts."
55. Cf. Czeslaw Milosz, *The Witness of Poetry* (Massachusetts: Harvard Univ. Press, 1983): "That sacred art of the Word, just because it springs forth from the sacred depths of Universal Being, appears to us as bound, more rigorously than any other mode of expression, to the spiritual and physical Movement of which it is a generator and a guide... Sacerdotal in prehistoric times epic at the moment of Greek colonial expansion, psychological and tragic at the decline of the dionysia, Christian, theological and sentimental in the Middle Ages, neoclassical since the beginning of the first spiritual and political revolution – namely the Renaissance – finally romantic... poetry has always followed, fully

aware of its terrible responsibilities, the mysterious movements of the great soul of the people..."

56. *Sri Aurobindo on Himself*, SABCL XXVI, p. 374.
57. Rilke quoted in J. B. Leishman's introduction to Rilke's *Duino Elegies* (London: Hogarth Press, 1952), p. 16.
58. Whitman quoted in Robert A. Durr, *Poetic Vision and the psychedelic Experience* (New York: Syracuse Univ. Press, 1970), p. 252n.
59. See *Fifteen French Poets*, ed., Douglas Parmee (London: Longman, 1974), p. 26.
60. AE. Dyson, ed., *Poetry Criticism and Practice: Developments Since the Symbolists*, Case Book (London: Macmillan, 1986), pp. 133-34.
61. Martin Heidegger, "Holderlin and the Essence of Poetry," *Existence and Being* (London: Vision Press, 1949), p. 304.
62. Erich Neumann, trans. Ralph Manheim, *Art and the Creative Unconscious* (London: Routledge & Kegan Paul, 1959), p. 130.
63. Quoted by V. K. Gokak in "Poetry and Modern Consciousness," *Sri Aurobindo Circle*, 10 (1954), p. 133.
64. Ibid.

CHAPTER 6

Conceptualising Poetic Futures: Visions and Variations

> That everything which comes into being must pass away; that all is fleeting, all is moving; that to exist is to be like the fountain and have a shape because one is never still – is the theme of all art because it is the texture of reality. Man is drawn to life because it moves from him; he has desires as ancient and punctual as the stars; love has a poignant sweetness and the young life pushes aside the old; these are the qualities of being as enduring as man. Man too must pass away.
>
> Christopher Caudwell, *Illusion and Reality,* Indian Edition New Delhi: People's Publishing House, 1945; rpt.1956.*p 316.*
>
> We live still in an age which is in a great intellectual trouble and ferment about life and the world and is developing enormously the human intelligence, often at the expense of other powers which are no less necessary to self- knowledge, in order to grapple with life and master it. We are seeking always and in many directions to decipher the enigma of things, the cryptogram of the worlds which we are set to read, and to decipher it by the aid of the intellect; and for the most part we are much too busy living and thinking to have leisure to be silent and see. – Sri Aurobindo, The Future Poetry.
>
> The world is a movement of God in His own being; we are the centres and knots of divine consciousness which sum up and support the process of His movement.... The world is a formula, a rhythm, a symbol system expressing God to Himself in His own consciousness. ("The Web of Yoga", SABCL, XVII, p.50)

There are of course several approaches to any given text; and hence in its own way Sri Aurobindo's *The Future Poetry,* affords several gates of entry. Conceived as early as the second decade of the twentieth century, its complete text bloomed forth only by 1930s. As was usual with him, he chiseled and shaped it as periodical chapters. By then he had settled down in his own ashram in Pondicherry, and was concurrently working on several articles and essays which would soon go into press as tomes on a variety of issues ranging through politics, philosophy, textual exegesis, interpretative readings, yoga and spirituality. There is arguably little doubt that the grand narratives of the nineteenth century were prime forces that churned out his intellectual exegeses. Having said that, it might not be out of place here to close-examine *the Future Poetry* alongside another great work on a similar scale like Christopher Caudwell's *Illusion and Reality*: *A Study of the Sources of Poetry* that was first published as early as 1937 immediately after its author's premature death at the age of thirty. To call Caudwell's work as great might be a bit odd in due consideration of its dogmatic tone and an over-eagerness of its almost juvenile author. Had he lived longer perhaps he could have carried out major alterations in the text. Nevertheless, both books show suitable evidence of their respective author's enthusiasm and desire for cutting new wood; both reveal ample intellectuality, and a strong desire for experimentation and amazing comparative scholarship. Both are testaments of applied close-reading and explorations of consciousness in their efforts towards creating a new poetics. But perhaps the comparisons and similarities would stop there; there are more dissimilarities that would surface when one places the two texts beside one another. But what intrigues me is the tremendous commitment and philosophical acumen shown by both the authors in tracing out their individual ideologies and applying this to the history of what appeared to them most significant at that point of time: the history of British poetry. Both Sri Aurobindo and Christopher Caudwell resort to the history of British poetry to establish their theories of evolving poetic consciousness. This could be the common point of departure for our inquiries as well. But however, the intention of this essay is not to draw parallels and establish identities but instead to *explore possible parallels* and inquire into *difference* and *insights*.

Many of those who read this essay could certainly be familiar with the life and work of Sri Aurobindo, however, it is likely that they may not be that familiar with Caudwell's *Illusion and Reality* or *Studies in a Dying Culture* or *Further Studies in a Dying Culture.* Hence I begin with a brief foray into Caudwell.

A short introduction to Christopher Caudwell *(20th October 1907 – 12th February 1937)*

Christopher Caudwell was born in London in 1907 and christened Christopher St John Sprigg. He left school and started work as a journalist at 15. He was a voracious reader and delved into philosophy, sociology, anthropology, psychology, history, politics, linguistics, mathematics, economics, physics, biology, neurology, literature and literary criticism and much more. At the age of 27, Caudwell became interested in Marxism and began his study of it with extraordinary intensity, discovering that it provided the key to the synthesis he was seeking. He wrote *Illusion and Reality* in 1935. He was killed in action while fighting in the Spanish civil war. (Some relevant details of his major works have been provided at the end of this essay).

One of his own contemporaries Ellen Sypher writes:

> He was and remains more or less of a maverick. From upper middle class roots, he left school at fifteen to work in aeronautics. After his commitment to Marxism he moved to Poplar, a working class section of London, where he wrote and did menial party work for the British Communist Party, whose leadership did not even know of him until after his death. He apparently undertook his serious theoretical work in isolation. His work bears all the weaknesses of such an individualistic position in that he uncritically accepts prevailing attitudes. Especially he ignores proletarian culture, and he depends too much on the then very influential Freud. Yet notwithstanding these narrow dimensions of his work, some of his perceptions of literature's basis and workings stand alongside those of the best of Marxist aestheticians. Caudwell's work, undoubtedly because of its mixed character, has not substantially influenced any writer on aesthetics although he is undisputedly the major Marxist writer on aesthetics in the British and U.S. tradition.

The point that leaves us worrying is the one about Caudwell's elusive legacy, probably on account of his eclectic and "mixed character". But then there is little doubt that he was an important intellectual who thought in new lines. Now, about his *Illusion and Reality*, the critical world conveniently sidelined. Even his own latter day Marxist lineage condemned him as having engaged with *vulgar Marxism*!

> As Marxist Literary theory underwent a 'cultural turn,' Illusion and Reality was increasingly seen as dogmatic and rigid in its discussion of bourgeois poetry. The debate shifted away from its use of Freudian concepts to its ties with Stalinist Marxism. In Culture and Society (1958), Raymond Williams said of Illusion and Reality that it had "little to say of actual literature that is even interesting" and that the book "is not even specific enough to be wrong." Terry Eagleton remarked about Caudwell in 1976 that "there is little, except negatively, to be learnt from him." Even E. P. Thompson, one of Caudwell's most generous late-interpreters, argued that the status of Illusion and Reality should be downgraded among Caudwell's works in favor of Studies in a Dying Culture (1938).From the late 1950s until the late 1980s, Illusion and Reality was equated with vulgar

Marxism. However, Christopher Pawling's 1989 book on Caudwell sought to restore the reputation of Illusion and Reality by suggesting that it belongs to what Raymond Williams called an "alternative Marxist tradition" that included Antonio Gramsci, George Lukács, and Lucien Goldmann.

There are two major theoretical positions that constitute the backbone of Caudwell's arguments – Marxist historical materialism and IA Richards' formalist methodology reflected through *New Criticism*. Caudwell's own reading of Marxism apparently is of the textual kind and he applies its logic and methodology almost religiously to his interpretation of poetry and poetics, as strongly condemned by later Marxists themselves. For him sociology formed the study of primary human relations and the theory of historical materialism is a palpable and verifiable truth of life. We read at the beginning of his classic text:

> Concrete living is not solid crystal. At any one time men are doing different things and therefore stand in relation to one another. The study of these human relations in a general form is sociology. This sum of human relations is not changeless in time but changes rapidly. The general laws determining the relations of human beings at a given period, and the change of these relations from period to period, form the theory of historical materialism.

At the very outset he rejects idealism as emotionalism and incapable of aiding in the understanding of poetics.

> As regards this study of poetry, we reject from the outset any limitation to purely aesthetic categories. If anyone wishes to remain entirely in the province of aesthetics, then he should remain either a creator or an appreciator of art works. Only in this limited field is aesthetics "pure."

And he continues:

> But as soon as one passes from the enjoyment or creation of art works to the criticism of art, then it is plain that one passes outside art, that one begins to look at it from "outside." But what is outside art? Art is the product of society, as the pearl is the product of the oyster, and to stand outside art is to stand inside society. The criticism of art differs from pure enjoyment or creation in that it contains a sociological component. In art criticism, values are ranged and integrated in a perspective or world-view which is a more general view of art from outside. It is an active view, implying an active living relation to art and not a cold contemplation of it, and implying therefore a view of art as active, with an explosive, energetic content. And it is a view of art, not of society or of the mind.

For Caudwell poetry is one of the earliest aesthetic activities of the human mind. But however fundamental to his poetics is the faith that poetry is founded on the economics of the times. Because, as he visualises it, poetry is the nascent self-consciousness of man, not as an individual but as sharer with others of a whole world of common emotion.

> Therefore the phantastic world of poetic ritual, myth or drama expresses a social truth, a truth about the instincts of man as they fare, not in biological or individual experience, but in associated experience. Such truths are necessarily phrased therefore in the language of the emotions. A pianola roll is pierced with holes. Those holes are real concrete entities. But they are not the music. The music is what happens when it is played. The poem is what happens when it is read. (22)

According to him, it is impossible to understand modern poetry unless we understand it historically – in motion. We can only bring back dead formulae from a study of poetry as static "works of art," something frozen and ossified. This is particularly true where poetry is the organic product of a whole society violently in motion. And this is how he sees the process of the birth of poetry:

> The birth of poetry took place from the undifferentiated matrix of the tribe, which gave it a mythological character. It separated itself from religion as the art of a ruling class in class society, but, except in moments of revolutionary transition like that of fourth century B.C. Greece, this art led a quiet existence, mirroring the slow rise and slow collapse of a class "whose first condition of existence is conservation of its mode of production in unaltered form." Then a class developed beneath the quiet, stiff art of feudalism, whose vigour is first announced by the Gothic cathedrals. This class in turn became a ruling class, but one whose condition of existence is a constant revolution of the means of production, and thereby the relations of production, and with them the whole relations of society.(50)

Poetry is so intricately connected to social structures as he sees it, and in its evolution we can trace the evolutionary map of social relations as well. Now as we have seen from the above brief discussions Christopher Caudwell is a committed Marxist theoretician and his methodology is so clear and well defined: it is an analysis based on societal productivity and class differences, absolutely textual. Poetry is not for him an individual activity. But a social engagement. However poetic activity is a liberating one: it liberates the poet and human consciousness. There is also a significant chunk of Freud in Caudwell's reading of British poets. Perhaps here is a pleasant point of intersection between these two cardinal texts of aesthetics, *Illusion and Reality* and The *Future Poetry*. Both are sort of primers in their own manner. Let's turn to Sri Aurobindo.

Aesthetics as it is generally understood is the pursuit of beauty. It is the study of sensory experience as visualised by the 17th and 18th century European thinkers. However, over the years the aesthetic has come to occupy a significant position in our understanding of the world and our place in it socially and historically and culturally. The Sanskrit aestheticians not only have contributed to the historical positioning or horizontal development of the aesthetic, but also have done great work in conceptualising the axiological values in a vertical axis, or the cultural matrix in specific locations of time and place. The history of the aesthetic is certainly linked to the history of place, culture and human memory. In the line of the Vedic, Upanishadic and later Puranic contexts the aesthetic occurs in the locus of our inward living. *Satyam Sivam Sundaram* – these are three nodes that constitute the entire created cosmos. And they are the quality of the Spirit that inhabits the self and the universe at once immanent and transcendental. In Sri Aurobindo's vision the world is a playground of the Spirit in its unfolding. [1]

We must remember that Sri Aurobindo never gave up writing poetry or reflecting upon it at any point in his life. Poetry for him was the index of the evolving consciousness. He had a strong faith in the transforming potentialities of the mantra or the word. *The Future Poetry* and the innumerable letters on art, literature, and poetry in particular are testaments to this belief. Although in the line of the ancient law-givers he too believed that poetry could never become a substitute for *sadhana*, at every point in his yogic development he resorted to the aesthetic as a creative edifice for the god-ward becoming. *Rasasvadah Brahmasvada sahodarah.*

Sri Aurobindo had recognised that among the prime purposes of poetry there was *antaschamatkara* – or inner spiritual expression and

1 In his extremely interesting book *Zen and the Art of Motorcycle Maintenance,* Robert M Pirsig (1974; rpt. London: Corgi, 1981) attempts to develop a *theory of Quality* substituting this concept for religious notions like God or Spirit. His character Phaedrus at one point states categorically that, "*Quality is the Buddha,*" and argues "such an assertion, if true, provides a rational basis for a unification of three areas of human experience which are now disunited." (p.231).These three areas are *Religion, Art* and *Science.* If only we could reunite these three nodes, we could be on the right track. In many ways Sri Aurobindo's attempt was toward this direction of holism and unity.

enlightenment. He wrote in one of his innumerable letters on poetry: *I used Savitri as means of ascent....*

And he constantly rewrote much of what he wrote from new and newer insights gathered from yogic experience. In fact we could look upon *The Life Divine* as his philosophical theorising, *The Synthesis of Yoga* a sort of practical field guide, and *Savitri* as a poetic explication of the text of his yogic becoming. It is significant too that *Savitri* does not evince what he termed the *Supramental Transformation* but only endeavours to preface and contextualise it. However, to believe in the Upanishadic view: *raso vai sah*, Bliss verily is Brahman. And the bliss of the poetic is that charges the entire poem and its poetic structure. *The Future Poetry* forms the aesthetic text of Sri Aurobindo.

Whatever be its shortcomings or limitations when we approach it from our present over-theorised intellectual situation, *The Future Poetry* remains among the first few serious attempts towards the formulation of a comparative aesthetic – a dialogic engagement with the burden of European tradition that was ingressing into the psyche of a generation floundering on the threshold of self-identity, and another almost remote and alienated one in itself, but whose roots could still be salvaged. Perhaps, one of its paradoxes was that Sri Aurobindo chose to formulate his aesthetic in the language of the coloniser, and in more than one place, the discerning reader might feel a slight unease at his free and sometimes too frequently unrestrained movements between the English poetic tradition and the insights drawn largely from Indian sources. But such interreadings would serve to evidence the characteristic virtuosity of its author who was equally at home in the Latin, Anglo-saxon and Sanskritic poetic traditions. A close-reading of Sri Aurobindo would convince us that he lived with his aesthetic and metaphysical quests as we live with our everyday realities. Hence, it was not merely the urge to re-define a nationalistic tradition and validate its futuristic insights on the face of an oppressive cultural onslaught that resulted in *The Future Poetry,* but something more of a significant involvement with the larger questions of poetry and human life.

The text of *The Future Poetry* as we have it now runs into thirty two chapters inclusive of "Introductory" remarks and "Conclusion". The publishers' Note to the first edition, August 1953, says:

> "The Future Poetry" was first published as a series of essays in *the Arya* (from 15-12-1917 to 15-7-1920). Sri Aurobindo thought of revising it throughly before giving it the form of a book. He wished to add even a

few chapters, especially one dealing with the Metaphysicals. He was not able to do more than write a few paragraphs supplementary to matter already treated; these have been incorporated in their proper places in the present edition which is thus practically a reprint of the original essays. (*The Future Poetry,* Pondicherry: Sri Aurobindo Ashram, 1953).

It was indeed unfortunate that the author himself could not do a thorough revision of the text or at least supervise the publication in book form. These essays, spanning a period of about three years, we should remember, were written serially, amidst the thick of several other involvements, as monthly installments – but that doesn't reduce the coherence of the argument as a whole. However, when one recalls that the *Arya* was a periodical that Sri Aurobindo co-edited with the Richards, and it was a philosophico-religious journal devoted to the exposition of an integral view of life and existence, and also the fact that its life-span spreads from 15 August 1914 (when it was launched) to the last issue in 1921, enfolding within its pages Sri Aurobindo's major contributions, it would be only logical to argue that *The Future Poetry* should not be delinked from its author's other works – works in the field *M* philosophy, social history and Yoga. In fact, Sri Aurobindo's works are informed by an integral vision of life and spirituality. And *The Future Poetry* is no exception.

The first five chapters set forth the context of Sri Aurobindo's arguments and theorise on his notion of poetry as Mantra. The next is an inter-chapter that centers on his view of the national evolution of poetry, and the following seventeen chapters constitute a historicised reading of English poetry from Chaucer to Yeats and A.E. Chapter twenty four is again an interchapter and it gathers the earlier arguments together to focus on what is to follow. Chapter twenty five to thirty two, attempt towards a reinstating of Sri Aurobindo's vision of poetry and are a vibrant exposition of what in his terms form the hieratic quincunx – the five suns of poetry: Truth, Beauty, Delight, Life and the Spirit.

As part of the Sri Aurobindo Birth Centenary Library editions *The Future Poetry* was reissued in 1972 and it incorporated the bulk of his letters on poetry, life and art too. In 1983 the Aurobindo Ashram brought out the second edition that claimed to be "the full-revised text" having undergone thorough checking against the author's manuscript. In this text the contents have been arranged in two parts, with certain Appendices, list of emendations, glossary etc.: the major change being the retitling of the Introductory Chapter into "The Mantra".

It is this second edition of *The Future Poetry* that I have used for the purposes of the reading that follows.

The immediate context of Sri Aurobindo's treatise was a book by James H. Cousins, *New Ways in English Literature* (Madras: Ganesh & Co., 1917), which was sent to him for review in the *Arya.* He soon abandoned the review idea and set out on a work of larger scope in which he thought he could develop his "own ideas and his already conceived view of Art and Life" (Editor's Note, 1983).

In the introductory chapter "The Mantra", Sri Aurobindo notes that Cousin's book raises problems which go beyond the strict limits of the author's concern and "suggests the whole question of the future of poetry...the higher functions open to it." He goes on to say:

> Taking the impression it [Cousin's book] creates for a starting point and the trend of English poetry for our main text, but casting our view further back into the past, we may try to sound what the future has to give us through the medium of the poetic mind and its power of creation and interpretation. (9)

Thus Sri Aurobindo's concerns are quiet clear; a re-reading of the past and immediate present with an insight gained from an understanding of both European and Indie traditions, and consequently to postulate on the future course of poetry.

Although there is no conscious attempt here to formulate an aesthetic system as such, in the sense of a philosophy of beauty, one could find in the course of the argument an implied psychology of aesthetic experience: one that informs Sri Aurobindo's life and work alike, and a historicisation of it.

Sri Aurobindo was quite familiar with the span of Western critical tradition from Aristotle up to T.S. Eliot, and more particularly the English critical tradition from Ben Jonson, Sydney and Dryden to the twentieth century, and also the Indian tradition with its emphasis on *rasa* and *dhvani* in the line of aestheticians like Bharata, Bhatta Nayaka, Mammata, Anandavardhana and Abhinavagupta – this *The Future Poetry* and the large number of letters on literature and art would stand testimony to. Being a radical visionary his preference or acceptance of any aesthetic proposition was not by mere intellectual agreement but by a deep intuitive insight which demanded harmony and integration rather than anything else. And his speculations on the aesthetic recognise the primacy of the spiritual, or in other words his is a "spiritualised aesthetic". All art, as Sri Aurobindo envisions it, in its own way, seeks to arrive at a concentrated expression of the Spirit, and it is from the *soul* that the expression originates and it is to the *soul* that it unveils the Real. Sri Aurobindo makes this clear at the outset itself:

> For neither the intelligence, the imagination, nor the ear are the true or at least the deepest or highest recipients of the poetic delight, even as they are not its true or highest creators; they are only its channels and instruments: *the true creator, the true hearer is the soul* [my emphasis]. (11)

Now this might sound neo-Platonic, but when one reconsiders Sri Aurobindo's sources – the *prasthanathrayi,* the Vedas, Upanishads and the Gita – it becomes clear that his is a vision at one with an alternative tradition that recognises the validity of the Spiritual at the heart of being.

To believe his own asseverations, it was an "experiential realisation" that confirmed his vision of the essence of all things as the Infinite Divine Truth of Being, at once conscious, and divine – *Satchitananda (Sat:* existence; *chit:* consciousness; *ananda:* bliss). And the aesthetics that underlies *The Future Poetry,* as I have pointed out, is an aesthetics implied in the creative experience of reality.

In the Aurobindian scheme of things, the *Soul* is the divine element in man that constitutes the aesthetic being, exulting and expanding in consciousness by God-ward experience, rising on its own curve to its divine consummation. Elsewhere he writes: "To find the highest beauty is to find God; to reveal, to embody, to create, as we say, highest beauty is to bring out of our souls the living image and power of God." *(The Human Cycle,* Sri Aurobindo Birth Centenary Library XV, p. 135).

Thus the Soul is the *antardtman,* the inner self, the true creator and recipient of the aesthetic delight or *ananda,* which in the language of Indian spirituality, is the essential delight the Infinite feels in itself and in its creation. As Sri Aurobindo choses to explain it,

> The world is a movement of God in His own being; we are the centres and knots of divine consciousness which sum up and support the process of His movement.... The world is a formula, a rhythm, a symbol system expressing God to Himself in His own consciousness. ("The Web of Yoga", SABCL, XVII, p.50)

And here we can see Sri Aurobindo's principle of *ananda* which is cardinal to his aesthetics. It would also recall to mind the Nietzschean thesis that only as an aesthetic continuum can the universe be resolved. But for Sri Aurobindo this *ananda* is part of the eternal ontological order and further this forms a direct link with the *rasa* theory of art central to the Indian aesthetic tradition that postulates *rasa* as designating the totality of the aesthetic experience – the creative experience of the artist, the aesthetic relish of the *sahrdaya,* and the essence of the created real. Perhaps the only major difference that his thinking would proffer is that, as with everything else in his entire thought-system, there is no finality to the evolving aesthetic boundary, no resolution, until the entire cosmos is "spiritualised". In his vision the soul of man, like all phenomenal being, is in constant endeavour to evolve from its unfinished nature and get into a unity with the Spirit through its multiform manifestation and on many different planes. It is a constant becoming, an order of transcendence and transformation.

According to Sri Aurobindo, in art this endeavour reveals itself in a sort of evolution from the objective to the inward to the inmost spiritual – a constant labor of self-finding and engagement. In *The Future Poetry* it is this characteristic insight that he brings to bear on the history of poetry down the ages more specially English poetry.

Poetry, as we read in *The Future Poetry,* is an index to the evolving soul of man, and in history it is also an instrument of the evolutionary upsurge. This general evolution of the aesthetic consciousness within the organism of the race has its own natural periods or ages but it is necessarily not linear or sequential. Each nation, as Sri Aurobindo propounds, has or develops a spirit in its inner being a special *soul-form* and a law of its nature which determines the course of its evolution.

Although Sri Aurobindo was totally unaware of the transformation that was taking place in art and literature in Europe at that time, the inception of a Modernist aesthetics with its divided ego, and unhinged narratives, his reading of the history of English poetry with its marked shift towards what he calls "subjectivity" reveals the profundity of his insights: if instead of the dichotomy between the objective and the subjective he had substituted self-reflexivity that would have served to describe the temper of the age much more faithfully. Perhaps, as his book further serves to evidence, his interest was less in recording literary history faithfully, than in tracing out the larger forces at work beyond and behind man and nature.

As he argues, the law of progressively becoming conscious of oneself is one of the fundamental laws of human existence, and poetry too reflects this trail authentically. Extended a little beyond its specificity, this evolutionary curve of English poetry can be applied to a new reading of world poetry with Homer and Chaucer representing the *physical mind* of the race, Kalidasa and Shakespeare the vibrant *vital mind,* and Vyasa, Sophocles, Virgil and Dante the *intellectual mind* in the "rhythmic voyage of self-discovery of the human spirit."

Concluding his historical survey, Sri Aurobindo observes:

> The progress of poetry, as it has been viewed in these pages, has been an index of an advance of the cultural mind of humanity which has enlarged its scope by a constant raising of the scale of the soul's experience and has now risen to a great height and breadth of intellectual vision and activity, and the question is at present of the next step in the scale of ascension, and whether it can now be firmly taken or will be missed once more with a fall back to another retracing of the psychological circuit. (238)

The next step is the most decisive step, for that will determine the character and temper of the future. And in the scheme of Sri Aurobindo, "Spirit" is the next grade above the intellect, and therefore, the intellect of the race needs must open now to an awareness of the spiritual, "an illumined self-knowledge and God-knowledge a world-knowledge too which transmuted in the great light will spiritualise the whole view and motive of our existence" (239).

Now from the foregoing succinct version Sri Aurobindo's reading of the history of English poetry as it traces the graph of evolving human awareness might sound too metaphysical and vague; but one should keep in mind the fact that all this has been couched in an idiom that is non-Western and non-Eurocentric. We have seen how Sri Aurobindo's aim was not mere literary history but on the other hand, the survey of English poetry was only meant to serve as a map of an aesthetic evolution that dovetailed with his vision of the role of poetry as an index of evolving consciousness. And what remains to be highlighted is the amazing fact that he has not even once recoursed to any European source to substantiate his historical endeavours apart from starting off with Cousin's book, of course. *The Future Poetry* as the testament of the aesthetic unfolding of the human spirit has to be seen as an integral part of the entire Aurobindian system – his life, work and yoga alike. It might very well be read as the product of cultural encounter, of colonialism and the backlash of a colonised national ethos. Sri Aurobindo's attempt though riddled with paradoxes, like the recoursing to the colonizer's language, and even tracing the history of a foreign body of poetry, should be then seen in a different light. What Sri Aurobindo has done is to universalise and conceptualise at the same time certain problems of man's changing involvement with his consciousness and the world, occurring at a crucial point in the formation of nationalistic awareness, when a whole people were struggling to redeem themselves from their oppressive present, through a conscious recovery of their collective heritage and to find an identity through their colonial difference.

In Caudwell we read,

> It is plain that poetry may be judged in different ways; either by the importance of the manifest content, or by the vividness of the affective colouring. To a poet who brings a new portion of external reality into the ambit of poetry, we feel more gratitude than to one who brings the old stale manifest contents. But the first poet may be poor in the affective colour with which he soaks his piece of reality. It may be the old stale colouring, whereas our other poet, in spite of his conventional piece of reality, may achieve a new affective tone. Old poets, we shall judge almost entirely by their affective tone; their manifest contents have long belonged to our world of thought. Hence the apparent triteness of old poetry which yet is a great triteness. From new poets we demand new manifest contents and new affective colouring, for it is their function to give us new emotional attitudes to a new social environment. A poet who provides both to a high degree will be a good poet. A poet who brings into his net a vast amount of new reality to which he attaches a wide-ranging affective colouring we shall call a great poet, giving Shakespeare as an instance. Hence great poems are always long poems, just because of the quantity of reality they must include as manifest content. But the manifest content, whatever it is, is not the purpose of the poem. The purpose is the specific emotional organisation directed towards the manifest content and provided by the released affects. The affects are not "latent," as in dream; it is associated ideas which are suppressed to form the latent content. Just as the key to dream is a series of instinctive attitudes which provide the mechanism of dream-work, so the key to poetry is a cluster of suppressed pieces of external reality – a vague unconscious world of life-experience. (227)

His own reading of poetics is based on the Marxist maxim that freedom is the recognition of necessity. And in the context of visualising what the future would proffer he writes:

> Only when communism comes into being will the conception of equal "rights" pass from the fabric of the State, and the State, too, wither away.

> The very "right" of man to realise his freedom by association with others negates the bourgeois conception of equal right, which was the highest ethic to which bourgeois culture could aspire. Its average man was a reflection of the equalisation of labour power in the market. "From each, according to his powers; to each, according to his needs." When men's innate ability and desires vary, how could such a creed – that of communism – be compatible with equal rights? A right implies something exercised against another, and communism is a state of society in which material conditions no longer force man to be the enemy of man. (292)

History and political will as Caudwell saw would reach beyond and cast the State aside, as Marx saw it, *the State will wither away*. The free individual would create free poetry.

On the other hand, as his life and brief political career would show, Sri Aurobindo chose to identify with the most often unseen larger forces at work behind those that regulate history and politics of individuals. This could account for his sudden withdrawal from the action front to being the recluse at Pondicherry. Later when in his writings he equates silence and soul-force this is what he means. New, reflecting on the future of poetry, poet though he was, with a vigorous nationalistic temper, he could not, however at any point wish away the burden of the colonialised self in him. Neither could he blindly harp on an almost apathetic Indian aesthetic tradition – primarily, because it was never homogenous, and secondarily, it centered more on dramaturgy rather than poetics, and more important to his purpose, it lacked the dynamism and alacrity that is necessary for the spirit's unfolding. His reading of Indian tradition was founded on the Vedas, the Upanishads and the Gita, and in the aesthetic evolution of the race, he recognised the selfsame creatrix unfolding to itself.

In the light of Sri Aurobindo's interpretation, ancient Indian Vedic culture was founded on spiritual truth of being, and man's essential truth rendered itself not in the horizontal plane of his daily activities, but intercepted it at every point in a vertical infinitude. The Vedic *s'ruti* appeals to the *s'rotrasya srotram,* the Ear of the ear, and it is to the soul of the hearer that it is addressed. Both the Vedic rishis, and the creators of the Upanishads that followed, conceived of the Word as an icon of the Absolute, and what they strived for was yoga of sound and sense. This culture of sound was to command the attention of later Indian philosophers of language, like Mandana Mishra, Kumarila Bhatta, Abhinavagupta and Bhartrhari.

The Future Poetry is a personal aesthetic testimony. It includes history, metaphysics and poetic theory within its scope. It is proposition towards a new spiritual aesthetic founded on past and present alike. In the final analysis, whether one agrees with Sri Aurobindo's poetic *darsana,* his view of the role of poetry and the poet, or his highly personalised reading of English poetry or not, one cannot help being impressed by the thorough going logic of his arguments. Here we see both Plato and Aristotle rubbing shoulders with Yajnavalkya and the Vedic seers. In the characteristic self-assurance of the *drsta,* Sri Aurobindo who combines the *kavi* and *bhashyakar,* delineates the future course of the spirit of poetry, and towards the close of the book we read:

> It is in any case the shock upon each other of the oriental and occidental mentalities, on the one side the large spiritual mind and inward eye turned upon self and eternal realities, on the other the free inquiry of thought and the courage of the life energy assailing the earth and its problems that is creating the future and must be the parent of the poetry of the future. (270)

Perhaps, implied in such an argument, one could discern the radical dislodging of Eurocentric reference points. It might appear a rather oddly launched reductivistic thesis that sees the West and East in terms of intellect and intuition, the materialistic and the spiritual. But considering Sri Aurobindo's historical position and his contemporary situation and the terminology available to him, we should reinterpret this line of thinking in terms of the polemic of the post-colonial consciousness ideally seen by a futuristic visionary who has not glibly circumvented a cultural situation and value.

In Caudwell's theories poetry moves from primitive communist stage through feudalist and Capitalist phases. Divisions in social systems reveal the divisions in the structure of human labour.

The development of agricultural and pastoral civilisation leads to the creation of a ruling class which becomes ossified and has as its counterpart a class of serfs and slaves. The struggle with Nature is transformed into men's struggle with each other. The first emergence of the ruling class is seen as the transformation of mythology into the epic, and into story, and in the evolution of ritual into play. The conflict of society is reflected in a poetry sombre and clouded with moral issues – questions of right and wrong – balanced by a poetry concerned with delight – with love and joy. Doubt, pathos, nobility, serenity, fear and a conscious beauty all enter the field of poetry. And the development of classes, by rendering possible the differentiation of function, gives more freedom to individuality. For the first time men speak personally in poetry. The lyric is born. (309)

In his vision of future poetry, Caudwell sees the movement forward from bourgeois culture to communism, an increase in freedom. *It is a movement back to the collectivism and integrity of a society without coercion, where consciousness and freedom are equally shared by all.* (311) This is *perhaps that heaven of freedom* that Rabindranath Tagore evoked in his famed *Gitanjali.*

By way of a Clumsy Comparison

As I mentioned at the opening of this essay there are several exits and entrances. I have veered away from seeing Sri Aurobindo's efforts as an isolated one. His own framework of poetic futures encloses the history of British poetry that he was familiar with, and his reading envisages a possible expansion of consciousness. There is little doubt that here the sensitive eye and the attentive ear can sense the echoes of Hegelian dialectics and Bergson's idea of creative evolution. Such an evocation is definitely not to devalue the essence of the Aurobindian eye, but only an attempt to understand and see him in perspective, in the geography of his intellectual heritage and in the landscape of the history of ideas. Christopher Caudwell's attempt at engaging with the dominant ideology of his time also leads him to contextualise and reread the history of British poetry. *Illusion and Reality* is certainly a testament worth perusing for those interested in the history of poetry and the poetic of the future. The discerning reader open minded enough would certainly see the parallel movements of both texts – *Illusion and Reality* and The *Future Poetry*.

I have titled this section clumsy because of the obvious distance between the ideologies of both these authors and the texts chosen. *Illusion and Reality* is a classic instance of text book Marxism. Of course its young author was all too young for mature reflections on a topic like this and we also are informed that Caudwell wrote the entire book within a short while. His boyish enthusiasm and over excitement at exploring the psyche and fantasy connecting it to the creative aspect of poetry and thus evolving a new direction in literary aesthetics is so blatant in the form of the text as we have it. But Caudwell's "intention" is to out-reach his times and break new wood. In this context both he and Sri Aurobindo are revolutionaries and pioneers. Caudwell and Sri Aurobindo are both "*over-reachers*" who explored newer reaches of poetic analysis. Their chosen intention was to topple hitherto held reference points and with due respect to the mode and methods of analysis, tools and references available to them at the time of their launching their poetic testaments, we as discerning critical minds should honor their work, methodology and output. In the history of literary theorising *The Future Poetry* and *Illusion and Reality* are textual landmarks.

Works Cited

Note: *Sri Aurobindo's complete works have been produced by the Sri Aurobindo Ashram, Pondicherry, as Sri Aurobindo Birth Centenary Library (SABCL) in 1972, and they are constantly being corrected proof-read and updated* – a new complete edition is awaited.

Aurobindo, Sri. The Future Poetry,2nd Ed. Pondicherry: Sri Aurobindo Ashram, 1983.

Aurobindo, Sri. The Web of Yoga, Sri Aurobindo Birth Centenary Library. Vol. XVII. Pondicherry: Sri Aurobindo Ashram, 1972.

Aurobindo, Sri. The Human Cycle, Sri Aurobindo Birth Centenary Library. Vol.XV Pondicherry: Sri Aurobindo Ashram, 1972.

Aurobindo, Sri. Savitri: A Legend and a Symbol. 10th imprint. Pondicherry: Sri Aurobindo Ashram, 1984.

Cousins, James H. *New Ways in English Literature.* Madras:Ganesh & Co., 1917.

Caudwell, Christopher. *Illusion and Reality: A Study of the Sources of Poetry* (1937) 1945; rpt New Delhi: People's Publishing House, 1956.

Mukherji, Ramaranjan. *Literary Criticism in Ancient India.* Calcutta: Sanskrit Pustak Bhandar,1966.

Murali, S. *The Mantra of Vision: An Overview of Sri Aurobindo's Aesthetics.* Delhi: B R Publishers, 1997.

Murali, S. Tradition and Terrain: Aesthetic Continuities. Delhi: B R, 2007.

Murali,S. Sri Aurobindo's Aesthetics and Poetics: New Directions. Delhi: Authorspress, 2013.

Pirsig, Robert M. *Zen and the Art of Motorcycle Maintenance.* 1974; rpt. London: Corgi, 1981.

Raine, Kathleen. "*The Future Poetry,*" *Sri Aurobindo Circle*, 15, 1959.32-36.

Sypher, Ellen. "*Christopher Caudwell, His aesthetics and film,*" *Jump Cut*, no. 12/13, 1976, pp. 65-66.

Christopher Caudwell Primary Works

Collected Poems. Manchester: Carcanet: 1986; The Concept of Freedom. London: Lawrence and Wishart, 1977; The Crisis in Physics, edited with an introduction by Professor H[yman] Levy.

London: John Lane, 1939 [rpt 1949]; Illusion and Reality; a Study of the Sources of Poetry. New York: International Publishers, 1967.

Romance and Realism: A Study in English Bourgeois Literature, edited by Samuel Hynes. Princeton, N.J: Princeton University Press, 1970; Scenes and Actions: Unpublished Manuscripts, selected, edited, and introduced by Jean Duparc and David Margolies. London: New York: Routledge & Kegan Paul, 1986;

Studies and Further Studies in a Dying Culture, introduction by Sol Yurick. New York: Monthly Review Press, 1971. [Reprint of Studies in a Dying Culture (1938) & Further Studies in a Dying Culture (1949)] This My Hand [novel]. London: Hamish Hamilton, 1936

[He also published several books of crime fiction and on aeronautics under his real name.]

CHAPTER 7

On Reading Sri Aurobindo: Blindness, Insight, Outlook and a Perspective

A Prefatory Note

The subtitle of this piece would certainly recall the famed theoretical essay of the same name on the rhetoric of contemporary criticism by the American critic Paul de Man. However what follows is far from any hermeneutical exegesis or any interrogation into the protean fields of theory and counter-theory even in the Indian context. My intentions are merely only to gather together the con/text(s) of the Aurobindian texts as not-read by the ardent devotees, or on the other hand explicated by self-styled scholars and their collective blindness which could hamper any serious "reading" or "interpretative essay". Even introspection is stilled into submission and converted into being mere un-self-reflective survey. Sri Aurobindo needs to be read and those possibilities of reading never should be taken for granted. No amount of prescription could lead one to the truth of the text. All reading calls for a verification of the text against oneself and other texts.

This is an initial outline for perspective and should not be misjudged as a finality: that would amount to mistaking the map for the territory.

For the ardent devotee who casually or intentionally visits the Sri Aurobindo Ashram the works of Sri Aurobindo appear as manna from heaven to be lapped up unhesitatingly and perhaps later conveniently forgotten during the demands and involvements of other things. He or she may pick up these works ranging from political treatises through philosophical speculations, to poetry and interpretative spiritual ideologies, and often browse through them as desired or directed by another friend or devotee and pass on. And but for the increasing number of interested tourists and inquiring novices the serious preoccupations of the Ashram and the larger discourses that have evolved round the significant works of Sri Aurobindo would have remained largely unnoticed. That there is an increasing traffic drawn toward his notion of man-making and his own version of evolving spirituality certainly speaks volumes for the significance of Sri Aurobindo in the present. Nevertheless the question remains: how is he to be read, and what are the larger issues which still cling on to his discourses which might go to hamper the quality of understanding or even further the process of spiritual enlightenment and reasoning? How is he to be read in the light of new emergent philosophies and theoretical engagements in an ever-changing and complex intellectual present? Of course another significant question also surfaces side by side: why go to all these needless mind games, why not simply read him as many have always conveniently read him and allow the inner amplification of his own vision to do the other tasks? For the simple-minded this last option should certainly be enough but for the ardent seeker there is indeed a whole array of interrogations ensuing from an intense reading of Sri Aurobindo's version of spirituality.

Let us take these issues one by one. Because for the unquestioning reader nothing actually matters we will leave such a reader to his/her own fate. The situation of the inquisitive reader could be generally seen under two heads: those who have read only the works of Sri Aurobindo for the most and are drawn into his amazing vortex through and through, on account of the innumerable disciples and their coteries; and second, those who have read and assimilated a number of "other" stuff and are gravitating toward the master's superior brand of spirituality armed with queries and questions galore. Reading and re-reading Sri Aurobindo's own works for them then would be an act of enlightenment, and the second category of inquisitive readers would go on asking questions just like those early generation of ardent devotees who had the great fortune of the proximity of the master himself and his own direct presence in the answers delivered to them even otherwise.

Sri Aurobindo's works are indeed like a gold mine and they appear then as being endless and pure, exciting to the core. The delight is also equally endless. Little doubt that, however, unconditional swallowing of a text without placing it in a clear perspective or clarifying its various aspects critically amounts to no reading at all.

In fact, as the master himself points out, either the absence of a critical insight or the lack of inward vision would result in simple veneration or drastic dismissal. This also brings us to the situation of the self-styled unbeliever who dismisses the entire oeuvre of Sri

Aurobindo as crass non-sense significantly because they are the products of a different generation, belong to a different order of discourse, and they revolve around spirituality which is decried in an age of commercial capitalism and market economy. To corroborate their dismissal they would also draw parallels with the simple-minded consumer mentioned earlier who claims to be "illuminated" and "blessed" on simply visiting the Ashram at Pondicherry, praying for a few hours at the Samadhi, or elsewhere, and browsing through a book or two from off the shelves. There are of course innumerable poetasters also who read and "interpret" Sri Aurobindo in order to pick holes in his arguments and proffer them as critical interpretations! They hardly matter in the long run. Spirituality and critical enterprise sometimes appears to run counter too. How does one resolve these issues?

Now to return to the inquisitive reader. The works of Sri Aurobindo – the texts as we have them now – are increasing by the day, on account of the archival research that goes into it. The secondary or interpretative scholarship also is increasing alongside. There are also enterprising scholars who engage with the works of Sri Aurobindo for securing a PhD degree for themselves. Many of them stray into the master's works for want of anything else or simply on account of writing on an Indian author in English (the resource materials are also fairly vast indeed!) The range of Sri Aurobindo is such that he could satisfy any scholar in almost any field whatsoever. So then sociologists, historians, philosophers, literary theorists, psychologists, anthropologists, cultural theorists, Sanskriticians, Indic scholars, life scientists, cultural geographers – you name it, they are all there! There is nothing wrong, sinful, or clever about exposing the works of Sri Aurobindo to the inquiries of different disciplinary methodologies. This goes to prove the inexhaustibility of Sri Aurobindo's scholarship and contribution. But the moment some too enterprising devotee steps in and cautions the "unwary" and the "radical" thinker of stepping into mined territory, Sri Aurobindo scholarship suffers unduly.

For the most, even among those so called self-styled scholarly inquiries into Sri Aurobindo one finds little or no scholarship apart from what gets reflected from the master's own skill and vision. I would like to classify these sorts of forays in general into two sets: as mere descriptive essays, and interpretative monographs. The first type usually ends up quoting Sri Aurobindo in large chunks and leaving the quotes as self-explanatory. The examiners also would find it easy to sanction degrees and diplomas to these "devotional" scholars and their dissertations unquestioningly. The second type would bring in some comparative elements quite tentatively and with great care for fear of crushing the master's words (quite unwarranted, no doubt!) and make sure that Sri Aurobindo's position is uniquely preserved even in the course of the textual arguments. These self-styled scholars then parade as arch Aurobindonians never ever casting a single glance at either Sri Aurobindo's works or their own (mis)readings ever afterwards.

Sri Aurobindo might be his own interpreter or rather his works could stand testimony to their own insights – but scholarship is indeed something more demanding than submissive commentaries, surreptitious asides, or supportive descriptions. Considering the fact that Sri Aurobindo himself was a master at critical thinking and encouraged anyone who came under his spell to further the intellectual realm, these self-professed Aurobindonians are wont to cause more damage than necessary. Sri Aurobindo certainly is a demanding intellectual, a radical mystic, who needs to be taken a little more seriously rather than left to defend himself in these so-called critical dissertations which are nowhere near to what he himself would have acceded to.

Over the last four decades after the birth centenary volumes (SABCL) were released, scholarship in and around Sri Aurobindo studies have certainly increased many folds. However, I am yet to come across evidences of critical writing of the level of a Sisir Kumar Ghose or a K D Sethna or a Srinivasa Iyengar. I, for one, had the good fortune as a young research scholar in the eighties to interact in person with these extraordinary giants in the field of Sri Aurobindo scholarship. K D Sethna impressed me with his amazingly broad sweep of influences and perspicacious brain. He never let go of his reading even after he came to settle in the precincts of the Ashram. Sisir Kumar Ghose on the other hand was a sort of peripatetic scholar who gravitated to Sri Aurobindo after a considerable stint with Alduous Huxley and later at Shantiniketan with the Gurudev. My conversations with him reminded me of dialogues with Aristotle or Coleridge or Harold Bloom. Srinivasa Iyengar had read researched and taught English literature before coming under the blinding light of Sri Aurobindo. His monumental biography is a piece of well-researched work that proffers a no-

nonsense background to Sri Aurobindo studies. Above all this soft-spoken academic was as erudite as ever on several levels at the same time. What mattered in the case of these three early intellectuals and academics were that they kept a steady head in the face of critical inquiry. Sethna moved among the works of Sri Aurobindo with the eye of a classical scholar, Iyengar read and argued with the tenor of a comparatist, and Ghose brought metaesthetic dimensions to the entire discourse. Granted Sri Aurobindo is a visionary who sought yogic sanction in all his pursuits and thereby it might be mandatory for an equally ardent follower to practice yoga rather than intellectually engage with his teaching in order to reach that spiritual realisation which the less-fortunate scholar might only cerebrally conceive. So then, we need to keep in mind the fact that there are these two broad segments – the simple minded devotee and the inquiring scholar. Four decades of Sri Aurobindo scholarship had produced perhaps a mere handful of significant works, free from mere rehash or simple citation, and even less genuinely concerned scholars.

As we have seen one of the biggest impediments in Sri Aurobindo scholarship had been the fact that the master's words themselves have been the most adequate explication of his vision. All one had to do was to put one's hand into the complete works or whatever, and pull out the gold vein – the rest will follow suit. For the unwary, no interpretation, no critical inquiry, no comparative reasoning – all it requires is the setting up of a string of citations and quotations, and parade them as one's own finding! How embarrassing! How unethical! The early scholars had their job well cut out – they had to read and interpret Sri Aurobindo in the light of critical and clearheaded thinking. The later scholars follow suit – the difference being the significant lack of critical reasoning. In Tamil they speak of grinding the already ground dough – in similar scale Aurobindo scholarship has deteriorated to mere rehash and thus lifeless and practically dead.

Citing the master's words themselves is one thing, but allowing someone else to speak on his behalf is another. For those schooled in English writing Iyengar and Sethna appear to offer the ultimate, and A.B Purani and sometimes Nolini Kanta Gupta, or Prema Nandakumar, could casually get thrown in. The worst form of torture is when some "spinelessly insightless" critics are paraded as having said this or written that when all they had done would have been to draw extensively from Sri Aurobindo's own writings. Isn't it silly and insipid to claim that one has quoted the master at length and thus arrived at academic Nirvana? Isn't it even *more sillier* and *stupider* to cite such rehashed chunks as corroborative evidence? *Perspicacious readers like Sisir Kumar Ghose, Sethna, and Prema Nandakumar would have spent sumptuous hours battling with the master's words racking their brains out before making themselves bold enough for borrowing those as evidences of what they want to establish.* When seen along the likes of Homer and Dante and Shakespeare if Sri Aurobindo's poetry holds up on its own then certainly it is worth perusing. When compared and contrasted with a volley of writers and intellectuals who had lived alongside him Sri Aurobindo's works are worth enquiring into, that should give us enough reason for delving in on our own. Either way mere rehash or sheer quotation should never compensate for direct encounter and inquiry. Political thought and action, historical reasoning and interpretation, philological exegesis and practice, philosophical inquiry and spiritual exploration, poetics and textual interpretation are all the characteristic strengths of Sri Aurobindo the visionary, and to neglect these in favour of citing someone who has merely lifted the masters own words as an authority, is to turn a blind eye to that critical inquiry which Sri Aurobindo himself stood for always. Of course it is not for all and sundry to interpret for oneself – that is a demanding task even for the demigods!

This brings me to the crux of my arguments: blindness, insight, outlook and finally a holistic perspective. In the early eighties when I was taking up my studies on Sri Aurobindo, CD Narasimhaiah, the doyen of Indian English scholars who established a unique centre for indigenous research in what came to be identified as postcolonial studies later (*Dhvanyaloka*, in Mysore) asked me quite derisively if I could cite some instances of poetry in the entire oeuvre of Sri Aurobindo. He himself had been brought up under the long shadow of New Criticism having studied at Cambridge with F.R Leavis and other eminent scholars of his times, and wont to question everything from the point of view of form narrative and practice. I had to resort to several instances from the poetry of Sri Aurobindo in order to convince the eminent professor that there could be other levels of poetry as different from the *Eurocentric* that he was quite familiar with. Such was the leniency of scholarship that resided in CDN that he was willing to listen and comprehend from a younger scholar – and accept many things which he would later argue about! Sri

Aurobindo's poetry we had come to realise by then had another level that required a different set of responses. Later CDN would write of *Savitri*, "if poetry is a mode of meditation, *dhyanamantra* you would find it here" (CDN, 1987) What Sri Aurobindo's works demanded for a clearer appreciation was an approach that was non-Eurocentric and at the same time a little different from that prevalent in those times. And only those among the innumerable self-styled arch-defenders of an overtly Indian perspective who could evolve an outlook that deviated from the dominant modernist vision could gather the required sensibility for responding to his works. While poets as different in outlook as Kathleen Raine and V K Gokak could read new lines and evolving directions in Sri Aurobindo, Indian modernists like P Lal and Nissim Ezekiel dismissed his work as derivative and deplorable. The issue then would certainly have been not the text of Sri Aurobindo but the contexts in which they were hyped and re-presented by the discourse of the spiritual which had by then overtaken and wrapped up the works themselves. New Indian sensibilities demanded the shedding of all that was debilitating and undermining, and the over dramatisation of the spiritual in all its ignorance by the non-initiated led to the growing intolerance of the ostensible ornamentation of all that metaphysical stuff of unreason. The tremendous impact of west-centric modernist discourses wiped out whatever indigenous sensibilities still residually clung to the Indian mind. All reading was modified under the light of new scholarship, under new reason.

Blindness resulted. The Ashram and his followers were closing down. After the great dawn of awakening that came to be recognised as the Indian Renaissance which never took off afterwards and was never even allowed to come to its logical conclusion, a great night of insensitivity descended. Scholarship in Sri Aurobindo studies came to mean only those sanctioned by the devout and the so-called saintly. The scribbles from the margin and from other discourses were silenced under the great arch of the Aurobindonians that was built of solid rock and guaranteed the faithful salvation and nirvana while the unfaithful rampaged on the outskirts as academics and intellectuals, forever kept away from following the silent pilgrim into the interior of *supramental manifestation*.

The film maker John Abraham a long time ago in a jovial mood told me that he had once explored the possibility of working on a documentary on Sri Aurobindo. After days of shooting in and around the Ashram in Pondicherry he moved over back home to the studio to develop the rushes of the film (remember those were good old days of the non-digital films!) Alas to his dismay he found all that he had shot had been overexposed in the "supramental glare of the Maharishi."

These are of course apocryphal, however, they lead us into the heart of what matters. The discourses that have crystallised around the work of Sri Aurobindo demarcated territories of reverence and desecration. As the poet had phrased it: *The death of the poet was kept from his poems*... (and) ...*the words of a dead man are modified in the guts of the living*. The works of Sri Aurobindo survived like Ishmael alone to tell the tale. They needed to be critically engaged with and their "truth" inquired into. But the first step in that direction had to be taken in the dark under the blinding light of the supramental! Well, too much of the sun can cause our too fragile sensibilities to warp and burn out. The followers of Sri Aurobindo's brand of spirituality rose and fell with the tide and turn of birthdays and *darshan* days schooled and tutored under scrupulous Gurus who interpreted the master's words suitably to the uninitiated. All that happened was a mere rehash of the words of the dead man. They were not allowed to germinate in the guts of the living for fear of the legendary doubts.

When someone speaks out there is a natural tendency to turn the blind eye. What is already known is always most welcome and what is interrogated and unearthed causes disturbances and so is neglected as irrelevant. The generally agreeable was the generally enjoyable. Insight was a laborious process that led to nowhere in particular.

Scholarship in Sri Aurobindo studies thus far had taken these directions: interpretative in terms of select texts and discourses specifically *recoursing* to acceptable readings. Comparatist perceptions like those afforded by Prema Nandakumar or Rhoda P LeCocq or Harold Coward had endeavoured to open up new directions in critical thinking but did not sustain sufficient support afterwards from elsewhere. Manoj Das, Rohit Mehta, Haridas Chaudhuri and Kishore Gandhi sought higher correspondences from Indic and non-Eurocentric directions, but the foundations they built up were rehashed by the next generation of scholars as dissertations and newer studies. The early generation of scholars had the guts to make new inroads while the later generation felt comfortable in sticking to the known and the predictable. There is an Arabian proverb that goes like this: *Traveller, there is no path; paths are made by walking.* Now to break new wood one has to await the strayed reveler. However, the strangeness of the territory is such that even the castaways are camouflaged and submerged. In this mire of the spiritual to build a fire one needed to get away first. All fires have died out.

The living spirit of inquiry that Sri Aurobindo so carefully preserved and cultivated appears to be misplaced. Vision, experiment and experience had been the catch words of the master both in his creative writing as well as in his philosophical inquiry (he was equally creative in both realms). But the quality of experimentation has begun to ebb away and along with it that special insight which is the inward eye of the initiate.

ON Himself:

> I had no urge toward spirituality in me, I developed spirituality. I was incapable of understanding metaphysics, I developed into a philosopher. I had no eye for painting – I developed it by Yoga. I transformed my nature from what it was to what it was not. I did it by a special manner, not by a miracle and I did it to show what could be done and how it could be done. I did not do it out of any personal necessity of my own or by a miracle without any process. I say that if it is not so, then my Yoga is useless and my life was a mistake – a mere absurd freak of Nature without meaning or consequence. You all seem to think it a great compliment to me to say that what I have done has no meaning for anybody except myself – it is the most damaging criticism on my work that could be made. I also did not do it by myself, if you mean by myself the Aurobindo that was. He did it by the help of Krishna and the Divine Shakti. I had help from human sources also.
>
> p.148-9 (13-2-1935)

> It was not any such thing [about the intellect] before I started the Yoga. I started the Yoga in 1904 and all my work except some poetry was done afterwards. Moreover, my intelligence was inborn and so far as it grew before the Yoga, it was not by training but by a wide haphazard activity developing ideas from all things read, seen or experienced.
>
> p.222 (13-11-1936)

The genuineness of the man and his single minded commitment are so superhuman that we have hard time considering that Sri Aurobindo was human after all. Anything that appears to call for a little more effort than was normal we humans ascribe to the divine and thus turn our blind spots into auras of admiration and adoration. This is nothing but sheer marginalisation and isolation of the more enterprising among us. History reveals what we humans have done to such greats almost at all times irrespective of geography and culture. Thus what we achieve by our blindness is loss of insight and that profounder perception – that will to achieve.

However, as Sri Aurobindo asserts:

> Impossible is our mask of things to be
> Mortal the road to immortality.
>
> (Sonnets from Manuscripts, c. 1934 – 1947)

We have identified several overlapping circles of discourse here. The primary one is that aura of *Supermind* which may or may not have descended. There are those determined disciples who would love to hang on to the nebulous godhead that lies like a nimbus round Sri Aurobindo. There remains little doubt that he was a guru of extraordinary powers and will. Few people have achieved what he did in his time. But disability to engage intellectually with his works amounts to indifference and insensitivity to the higher demands of spirituality. What he achieved was definitely through a solemn struggle – a product of cultural history that he himself was. The secondary factor which is no less significant is the one of his textual works which are also thereby clouded by "faith" and "belief" on one side and there by placed in a unique position of unquestionable authority. On the other side as we have seen they inculcate blindness. Sanctified by the establishment of devoted believers whatever goes for interpretation is mere rehash of his own words. Any efforts toward a critical vision or any element of debate and interrogation is viewed with sheer culpability and thereby corruption of the devotee's mind. Many are the ardent devotees who flock to the works of this supreme master of Yoga – they genuinely seek solace and comfort from the travails and traumas of this world. Several are the seekers who do indeed find their desired peace. They do not wish to be disturbed. They are blissful and at peace. Let us leave them to their own fate. Then there are these arch critics of Sri Aurobindo who target his works and the entire discourse that has sprung around the ashram and mock and deride the devout followers: for them this collective act of worship around tombs and *samadhis* appears silly and absurd. Their prejudiced eyes and biased visions proffer them only darkness and murk. They are thus innately blind. Let us leave them also to their sorry fates. He doesn't need us to defend him from the bulldozers of mockery and derision. His was a passion for the infinite and the beyond.

But there is an element of struggle and quest in Sri Aurobindo's works which need to be taken quite seriously indeed. As we saw earlier he was a product of his times and the cultural and intellectual context of his becoming are there for us as leads to his process of thought and the formulation of his philosophy. We have to recognise that Sri Aurobindo was an intellectual and a philosopher – his works and words are ample evidences for this view. He was a poet and essentially one as he himself has vouched. In fact as I have argued elsewhere his system of belief can be understood and resolved only as an aesthetic circuit with the human seeker on one end and the God head of the Spirit at the other end. So then this system would also require to be seen in the light of cultural and historical scholarship. Sri Aurobindo's life that is often recognised by many scholars as falling into three distinct phases begins with his European exposure and return to India and his political involvements leading finally to the withdrawn life of a seeker in Pondicherry. In all these three phases he had to encounter forces of decadence and degeneracy.

Let us take them one by one. His early upbringing by an anglophile father led to his over exposure to the aftereffects of the enlightenment rationality and an Anglo-Germanic philological heritage. His return to India was marked by a nagging self-doubt and an eagerness to identify with his non-Eurocentric self. This search for identity can be seen in his early political writing – the plethora of linguistic and cultural contexts that were reeling under a unifying colonial yoke afforded him the perspective toward a holistic synthesis, which leaves in itself a Hegelian trace. He was an activist and sought direct confrontation with the authority of the establishment. There are interesting exchanges between Sri Aurobindo and Mahatma Gandhi. Sri Aurobindo's withdrawal into French Pondicherry after his activist political stint reveals his desire for a synthesis of the intellect and the all enfolding spirit. He could envision the larger framework of cosmic action wherein the smallness and pettiness of little minds petered into insignificance. He was single minded in his pursuit of the spirit and a holistic transformation was his genuine desire. He was like the Buddha in that not until all life was on its way to be transformed will he let go, and individual nirvanas meant little for him. He devised a philosophy of spirituality and also evolved a map for the initiate to follow suit. The discourse that evolved later around all these contours is even now hanging like a smoke screen and his individual intellectual trajectory is almost already well lost.

Much like an Upanishadic seer that he was, he insisted his followers to engage with their own yogic experiences as he himself had done. He had of course many sides to his personality: the political thinker, the activist, the seeker, the yogi, the philosopher and the poet. Whatever preoccupations he went through he never let go of the last – that of the poet. Poetry afforded him the unique blending of inspiration and expression. The search for the mantra or that perfect unison of *sabda* and *artha*, sound and sense meant the quest for the ultimate unison of inspiration (vision) and expression (word). I used *Savitri* as means of ascension he wrote in a letter.

> I used Savitri as a means of ascension. I began with it on a certain mental level, each time I could reach a higher level I rewrote from that level... In fact Savitri has not been regarded by me as a poem to be written and finished, but as a field of experimentation to see how far poetry could be written from one's own yogic consciousness and how that could be made creative"

He wrote and reworked on the *Savitri* manuscript till his passing – the first canto alone had undergone thirteen revisions. Poetry for him worked as an index of the evolving human consciousness. His works are thus to be seen as maps of spiritual reading. To read them as holy words of the master is to behold their outer skeletal structure and like holding on to the shells of meaning. Let those ardent devotees clutch them for what they are worth but the master himself would have avowed that the not-so-simple minded at least trudge the narrow road of spiritual seeking and not be left in the blind alleys of adulation. Perhaps one of the major reasons for the intellectual stasis that is profoundly felt in the Sri Aurobindo circles today is on account of this blindness that withholds any possible insight. For the literary minded there is virtually god's plenty in Sri Aurobindo's works to spur them into comparative discussions and interrogations. For the philosophically inclined Sri Aurobinod has carved out new and newer niches of trajectories to be explored. For the spiritual minded the Integral Yoga that he has so painfully evolved in his own spiritual quest marked by eclecticism is left to be experimented upon and explored further.

Kishore Gandhi had experimented with the ideas of spiritual evolution in his works very much like the author of *Sri Aurobindo or the Adventure of Consciousness.* KD Sethna had ushered in comparative scholarship through his vast reading and Ghose had made new inroads with his *metaesthetic.* He had also drawn attention to the repeated misuse of the high-sounding *Aurbindonian* as an adjective and even suggested *Aurobindian* as a more modest alternate term instead. Haridas Chaudhuri and Frederic Spiegelberg tendered a forum for a dialogue and a symposium. Even in my own modest early book, *The Mantra of Vision*, I had attempted a holistic vision of the master Yogi and his creative work from an Indian perspective. Even in my later essay, entitled "Towards a Spiritual Aesthetics of the Environment: Quality, Space, and Being in Sri Aurobindo's *Savitri*," published in the US based journal, *ISLE Interdisciplinary Studies in Literature and Environment* Vol. 18. Issue 2 (Spring 2011) pp. 302-322 – I had visualised a unique perspective in terms of ecological dimensions and thus pioneered a new dimension in Sri Aurobindo criticism. In *Savitri Bhavan*, the poet and visionary Shraddhavan appears to have given a new direction to re-reading Sri Aurobindo while in the collective enterprise of SACAR under the direction of Ananda Reddy, serious interest in Sri Aurobindo scholarship appears to be flourishing. Their occasional seminars and workshops favour some sort of self-reflexivity. Many years ago Sreenivasa Iyengar and Prema Nandakumar had set Sri Aurobindo's writing in the intellectual perspective and larger framework of Indian writing in English to be explored and furthered by the next generation of scholars. Alas, the genuine scholar like the genuine devotee is a far cry in the present. Our times are marked by amazing changes and advancement in science and technology, the world we live in the present is definitely much more "advanced" than the times of Sri Aurobindo when the imperial and colonial forces held potent and powerful sway over all and everything. The market economy of the capitalist present and its itinerant scholarship grounded on claims to information that is universally accessible have blinded the already blind human eye further. The dismissal and de-valuation of metanarratives of the last century have laid claim to a territory of panoramic ignorance. Knowledge is doubted and wisdom is sidelined. Information has risen to the centre stage. And ignorance is prided as wisdom it has indeed become folly to be wise and remain so. Had he lived on beyond his times, Sri Aurobindo would have charted out new directions in the present. He would have been like the child in the story yelling out that the emperor is truly naked. However, his residual presence and urgency of intellectual inquiry have been erased and silenced. His works are rehashed and his words echo down the long corridor of forgotten memory and a misplaced past. Nevertheless, the eternal eye that would have led the inquirer forward is not yet completely closed though. There is a tiny fraction of opening. So then all is not yet lost. What is required is a critical temperament and a truth-seeking perspective that would not wither in the face of opposition and inclement weather – an outlook that does not succumb to the comfort and convenience of the commonplace and the mediocrity. The grand narratives of yesteryears might be ignored by the postmodern present that prides in the here and now, however, profound questions relating to truth and meaning, the nexus of mind and matter, the interrelationship of nature and human nature, are bound to be tenaciously pursued by those minorities who chance to reflect on their own selves and identities. Perhaps, then, like in the *Dantesque* vision there would arise the spirit of the master himself to lead the genuine seeker even through *Inferno* and *Purgatory* to *Paradiso*. Sri Aurobindo realised early enough that his was a superhuman struggle, to redeem the true spiritual identity of all human kind, he also realised that he had to explore his own inner self continuously and ceaselessly in order to chart out his map for generations to follow suit. His works are genuine asseverations of both these aspects. For the convenience of the present day scholarship he genially assents to being ripped apart as a poet, a philosopher, a political and social thinker, a man of Indian Renaissance, a spiritual yogi who chartered the direct pathway for the divinisation of the human being, and a literary critic. In the contexts of contemporary criticism this could be termed as *dismemberment* and *dehumanisation* because the organic unity of the man and his work is dislocated. What usually happens when such piecemeal readings are indulged in is that sloppy mis-readings are flaunted as original findings! Believe me, there are research scholars who bring up amazingly imaginative topics like *Sri Aurobindo and Paulo Coelho,* simply because they find that the latter speaks about the mystical, and magical. There are others who lapse into "spiritualism" without even recognising the terminological distinctions of the term or its historical connotations. For the unwary, *magic, meta-magical themes, mysticism and spirituality* are just terms which are mutually interchangeable. The true spirit of critical enquiry has petered into shallow and superficial research – the requirements of the present also appear to be thus merely skin-deep. Now, like HG Wells's tale of the valley of the blind, all of us are made to believe that to be blind is truly natural and thus made to turn quizzically toward one suitably endowed with sight and vision. *Whither is sped the visionary gleam? Where is it, the glory and the dream?*

In one of his remarkable poems Sri Aurobindo has written:

Who was it that came to me in a boat made of dream-fire,
With his flame brow and his sun-gold body?
Melted was the silence into a sweet secret murmur,
"Do you come now? Is the heart's fire ready?"

Hidden in the recesses of the heart something shuddered,
It recalled all that the life's joy cherished,
Imaged the felicity it must leave lost forever,
And the boat passed and the gold god vanished.

Now within the hollowness of the world's breast inhabits -
For the love died and the old joy ended -
Void of a felicity that has fled, gone forever,
And the gold god and the dream boat come not.

The Dream Boat 1930, revised 1942

Is it too much to ask to keep the heart's fire ready to be able to greet the dream boat? But first we need the strength enough to dream and to recognise the boat as it comes in to our sight. Having misplaced it we end up dancing absurdly round in circles. The simpleminded get saturated with contentment and become complacent. Once our outlook gets changed and our doors of perception are cleansed the voice of Sri Aurobindo would reach us clear and undisturbed. And the seeker in us will be awakened to pursue that action from where we left off.

Appendices

1

In Praise of the Many

The Pondicherry University campus is a rich medley of green, yellow, brown and red. The last remains of what was once ecologically indigenous and native to these parts – a few flowering trees and bushes – give it the impression of a still green campus. The drying and dying vegetation periodically supplies the variant tones of yellow and brown, while the red earth lies bare and barren under the broad blue skies. The canopy of the blue skies can vary between steely ultramarine blue to intense turquoise, sometimes even a rich purple. There is no lack of colours turn wherever you might. Even the torrential tropical monsoons tag with them an array of multiple colours. These colours lend the otherwise drab academic campus a sprightliness and variety all the year around that would prod even the weariest academician to turn back into life with the satisfying realisation that life is worth living.

Over and above this drama of the elements there is this unending surprise of innumerable animal, bird, reptile, amphibian and insect life in these parts. Quite recently, when we were emptying out a cupboard which we had almost never opened in years, out trooped a huge scorpion with a pleasantly surprised look that there were us humans around at all! We all were dancing round it while the woman who helps us in odd jobs promptly plucked it off the ground with her broom and with the deftness of an IPL batsman landed it fair and square on the far away bushes – a perfect six!

We as a family do not encourage killing of any kind, neither do we support violence. I still recall that a decade and a half ago this campus was far greener and wilder than it is now when we could come across these large crustaceans a-plenty wandering freely around; the frightened security guards then often battered them to death screeching and howling like tribes of wild American Indians Hollywood style! They used to slaughter and squash any and every wild thing – one need not mention the notable species of poisonous snakes which for some reason or other are seen by every man and woman even outside this green campus, as enemy no 1. Snakes, centipedes and scorpions along with spiders and crabs have been mercilessly and systematically eradicated from our part of the world over the years, that now one can barely come across any of these known species about in these parts.

There were times, several years ago, when driving around the campus at night my car headlights have illumined the alarmed and frightened eyes of jack rabbits, jackals and civets, to mention only a few large mammals. There are many that if one were extremely lucky one can still tick off one's list. Insects and reptiles too are around albeit not in such large scale that they used to be in the early part of this century when we turned up here. Diversity in terms of plants, bushes, creepers and trees have also steadily depleted, as is the sad case elsewhere too.

Birds still add a bit of colour to the changing skies and earth in our campus. I have photographed several species of birds – some resident and others migrants – over the years. The point of it all is that the entire campus has been a rich web of colours forms and life. As it should be! Because nature thrives on diversity and variety. Biologically, as almost everyone would know by now, life abounds in its affluence mainly through such plenitude and diversity and the web of life is maintained through this unique spectrum of variety and multiplicity. There is in nature a specific place and a unique slot for each and every iota of life. *All for one and one for all*, as the creator of the famed three musketeers has phrased it!

We humans as the most successful and dominant species on this planet have risen above all other living and non-living creatures and through the building up of our cultural edifices have quartered and sectored all that is non-human. We have our sciences and our histories, our mathematics and measurements; we have named and catalogued and ordered and organised all that is under and over the sun. Through this systematic nomenclature we have ascertained our superior rights and privileges. More than anything through our culture and civilisation we have made and maintained divisions and subdivisions not only outside our spheres but also within our own kind. It is in this context that our history tends to rewrite all that is human and non-human, in terms of that abstract entity, "power!"

Our politicians in whose tainted hands we have entrusted the fate of our earth are hand in glove to retain and maintain their power.

Our political systems are even wilder. In fact it is our sad fate that it is our politics that decides our very being in the present – in our dealings among ourselves and in our relations with the rest of the earth. To put it differently, biologically we may be one, and ecologically too, we are interconnected but politically, socially, economically, we are different and are segregated. Sometimes it would be in the interests of the powers that be to maintain and cherish this difference, but in other situations beneficial to them they swipe off this difference to have their way!

For instance, the dominant political and economic discourse in our times is certainly dependent on the technological model of development. Science and technology have helped to create a world run like a machine. Indeed, for the common man and woman it would appear as if they are living in someone else's dreams! They simply do not have any choice – but to follow blindly the juggernaut of change.

Western intellectuals like Michael Foucault, Jacques Derrida, and Edward Said have offered perspectives of differences and diversities. They have pointed out the presence of the invisible aspect of power in the very centre of all! This fact has also been underlined albeit in a different mode by Indian intellectuals like Swami Vivekananda, Sri Aurobindo and Ramana Maharshi. For Foucault and Said the presence of power is practically invisible and ingrained into our thinking itself. The Italian intellectual Antonin Gramsci has a technical term for it – hegemony. This is the invisible intangible something that relentlessly forces us to accept many things for granted simply because they appear to be common sense! Now common sense is rather the most uncommon one among us, but very few would realise that fact. In the present globalised world the general feeling is that technology would provide us with everything that we would require – even air, water etc. that we are fast polluting and depleting. Globalisation thrives on homogenising everything – that is in a way making us all to fit into the same mould. An average middleclass Indian dresses like an American, eats like an American, speaks like an American and even feels proud in thinking like an American. Just imagine what would be the state of affairs in a few years when all the world is deprived of its diversity and a totalitarian one world emerges!

We Indians are as a rule used to uphold multiculturalism in our everyday living: we speak different languages, worship many gods, eat differently, dress differently, sing and dance differently, and yet when it comes to matters of nationalism we realise we are a nation of difference and diversity. In many ways this non-reductive multiplicity is what keeps us unified as a nation that has several years of culture and history. When we speak of unity in diversity, we do not intend the power of homogenising forces squeezing the living space between us; we understand our one ness and our differences. The Americans have come up with this idea of a salad bowl to symbolise this multiplicity. Perhaps we Indians have already been through this!

In Kerala they make a delicious dish with several vegetables boiled together – avial, it is called. Here the taste is distinct because the vegetables remain different and separate – *all for one and one for all.* Conservation and preservation of our environment is linked to the politics that is being played around us every day. When the terrorist bursts with the belt bomb all that is around also are shattered. When the dictatorial power totalises and maintains itself as the centre what is challenged and desiccated is the variety of other lives.

It is time we wake up to the reality of the present. All around us life is losing its diversity – bio diversity is fast depleting, the environment as we used to know it is crumbling away, while cultural diversity is slowly fading, and people are fighting each other for the wrong reasons; all the while the exploitative class is getting away with all this – and ultimately we humans are the losers. But only we are to blame for all this. It is our responsibility. We need to wake ourselves up before all of us fall into the same kind of sleep and all of us have the very same dreams! *Viva le differance! Long live plurality and diversity.* As Sri Aurobindo wrote in *The Life Divine,* even the supramental is infused with diversity:

> "A supramental or gnostic race of beings would not be a race made according to a single type, moulded in a single fixed pattern; for the law of the Supermind is unity fulfilled in diversity, and therefore there would be an infinite diversity in the manifestation of the gnostic consciousness although that consciousness would still be one in its basis, in its constitution, in its all-revealing and all-uniting order."

2

Iswara Sadhana and Iswara Sakshatkara

One day, not so long ago, my mother had taken her grandson (my son, who was quite young then) to the nearby temple in my native village- little realising herself that times had changed since she left and returned. The man at the gate of the *Shiva temple* stepped up officiously to inform them that the child had to remove his shirt in order to enter – a practice generally prevalent in Hindu temples all over Kerala (of course, chapels and shoes were never allowed). My mother then quite innocently asked him in the nicest of tones: *does he have to remove his knickers too*? The man gave her a look with eyes hotter and fiercer than Lord Shiva himself. My mother in her own childhood had grown up in the premises of the temple and as a child had used to play hide seek even inside the sanctum sanctorum. Gone are those days when one could do the worship oneself with *pushpam, phalam, thoyam* – flower, fruit, water. Now there are innumerable middlemen even between us and Iswara. And rules.

In another part of our village I recall there was a small Ganesha temple maintained and frequented by army personnel. The devout among them used to look after the *puja* etc. As the village grew into a small town and the neighborhood developed into a city, the temple worship grew tight and tighter with new set of rules and regulations. People have apparently so little memory and tend to think that the customs and manners prevalent at a given present were ever there like that. Few seem to notice the slow creeping in of rigidity and superstitions over the years. Now the army temple is a huge structure with its own governing body and systems. Ganesha might have departed a long time ago, I guess. Hindu temples these days are rife with ritual and customary practices most which would surprise anyone just a little older than thirty years – a period which usually marks out one generation from the next.

Worse still is the way the ritual cleaning of the idols in temples these days. I cannot recall when this practice began of draping the stone deity with clothes before cleansing the idol. It looks as if the pujaris are worried the deity would in the process be denuded before the devotee! One can imagine the south Indian artisan sculpting the form for adoration and worship with genuine feeling for the structure and figurine. The iconic figures for worship cast in bronze or *panchaloha* (a mixture consisting of gold, silver, brass, copper and iron) are essentially adorned in fine textures of imagined drapery. And to think that when being bathed the deity might appear nude to the ardent devotee is sheer ignorance and imbecility. (I have dealt with this issue of nudity and nakedness at length elsewhere in another essay). And even if the icons were to appear naked what then? The entire idea of *Iswara* or the personal god needs to be close examined a little here.

According to Tantric belief the forms worship can be seen variously under three heads: pasu, vira, dhyana. The earliest animal form – *pasu* – belongs to a lower state of evolution wherein human physical existence is emphasized. *Vira* stage is the one where emotional states come into play with ideas and ideals of heroism and acts of supreme heroic achievement. The third stage of *dhyana* is where the anthropomorphic forms and ideas of the earlier stages are *beyonded* into a finer awareness of the supreme. There is a general abandonment of the visually recognisable in favour of more abstraction as one goes over these stages.

As for the case of adoration and worship of the deity, it would be best to cite Sri Aurobindo at this point. In the *Synthesis of Yoga* we read:

> In ordinary religion this adoration wears the form of external worship and that again develops a most external form of ceremonial worship. This element is ordinarily necessary because the mass of men live in their physical minds, cannot realise anything except by the force of a physical symbol and cannot feel that they are living anything except by the force of a physical action.

He points out that *pasu*, the herd, the animal or physical being, is the lowest stage of its discipline, and says that *the purely or predominantly ceremonial adoration is the first step of this lowest part of the way*. When we grow higher or evolve spiritually we come to realise the purity or transformation of our own outer vision.

> The aim of Yoga being union, its beginning must always be a seeking after the Divine, a longing after some kind of touch, closeness or possession. ....When this comes on us, the adoration becomes always primarily an inner worship; we begin to make ourselves a temple of the Divine, our thoughts and feelings a constant prayer of aspiration and seeking, our whole life an external service and worship..... It does not follow that the outward worship will necessarily be dispensed with, but it will increasingly become only a physical expression or out-flowing of the inner devotion and adoration, the wave of the soul throwing itself out in speech and

symbolic act. [see Synthesis of Yoga Part 3: The Yoga of Divine Love Chapter iv The way of devotion http://intyoga.online.fr/bhakti.htm]

Of course for the simple minded there would always needs be temples and idols and for the awakened there would still be worship and devotion, however there would be a qualitative difference in the order of perception. As Sri Aurobindo phrases it so poetically: *the wave of the soul throwing itself out in speech and symbolic act.*

Devotion and surrender are nobler acts only possible when human beings grow inwards sufficiently enough to comprehend the higher speech acts of the soul. Until then we will always have these rabble worshippers making up memory, ceremony, and customary practices out of nothing.

There is a qualitative difference between *Iswara Sadhana* and *Iswara Sakshatkara.* The differences range from recognising the qualities of Iswara or the personal god through the paying of obeisance at the feet of the religious icon, toward the realisation of the divine in oneself (*atma saksatkara*) through the act of devotion and surrender to that final realisation of the spiritual oneness. That is the inward becoming that the Hindu religion aspires to, however much it is denigrated in its extreme practices in the present day temples. After all, religion is the arc of god-ward becoming and the human being is but always *to-be-blessed*!

3
The Quietness of things

There are among many things a touch of sadness as one leaves behind each day to wake up into another: this is the inevitability that is true for anyone willing enough to carry the burden of memory. The relationship with things, with thoughts, feelings, sensations, people and places – never in that order ever – this is what we understand as life lived with intensity. And of course life becomes meaningful in any sense only when we get rid of the remorse and misgivings that trap us back in nostalgia. Nevertheless what is life without memory? The true truth of existence is certainly in the burden of our mental constructions. And a nostalgia for the present albeit a contradiction in terms makes one alive a little more than the ordinary. For Socrates, the unexamined life was not worth living. And any self-examination sets forth a series of chain reactions – for memory moves through association rather than any logic, and there is no beginning or ending. Everything is a flux – memories and reflexions and the living experience of the real. Who can separate thoughts from sensation and idea from the actual? Like a torch moving through a dark cavern illuminating and flickering over things and shadows our self-consciousness moves through the spatio-temporal world. What is real? Those things out there or our sensations of them? Does our awareness occur after we sense anything or does it occur prior to the act of realisation? Perhaps these happen at the same time simultaneously?

Touch is among the prime senses of being alive – we touch at several levels. The skin that holds up the contours of our bodies in their physical state of being works wonders in terms of converting sense experiences with the outer world other than ourselves into felt experience inside ourselves. There are several physiological factors like nerves, blood vessels, and other tactile biological systems that come into play here alongside the spinal chord and the brain. True miracle these when one considers them in isolation, but when seen alongside the rest of the world out there one recognises the larger maps of existence and sensation. Like everything else we tend to look upon our world in terms of our own standards – normalising our size as standard and seeing others with relation to this as either larger or smaller than us. Perhaps it is not easy to comprehend that there are no true standards in the universe, nothing is in actuality created *per se* in terms of anything else although each tiny particle is dependent on another for its existence and being. Our sensations are largely dependent on our sense standards and executable sense organs – any failure or shortcoming in any aspect of any of these factors may result in misdirected apprehension. If we have a shortcoming our world as we sense it will have that shortcoming and we would unconsciously judge that as standard thereby perverting our very sense. Then how do we know whether the self-examination of our lives is in the right light? All things are quiet like the dark deep night and our self-consciousness passes by. We carry some remnants of our awareness with us as memories and reflexions. After all any consciousness is self-consciousness. And every real thing depends on the self-reflexion of some consciousness.

A long time ago I recall coming across a conundrum: if a tree falls so deep in a jungle with no one in the near vicinity will there be any sound? Sound is noise received as audible sensations in the living ear and converted through the living apparatus as such – there are certain specific *decibals* the range of within which only audible sounds are recognisable. Ranges below would be subsonic and ranges beyond supersonic. This is to recognise that there are sound waves beyond and below normal sense perceptions of these waves. We may not call them sounds, just like the *no-sound* that actually is an audible sound that the falling tree produces in empty space in the deep jungle. Until and unless a human or other living biologically sound ear is around to decipher these waves in their right senses in their own reach and level they do not become alive as sounds at all – they keep on travelling in space until they peter out and die. Sense perceptions are also like these. There is a real world that falls outside our sense perceptions: it may not be real for us it may not be in existence at all for us until and unless we strike a similar chord in the time and space scale that would make them actual and real. Which is to say that the world cares little for us. We live and we pass. Our pains our pleasures our dreams our desires and longings are of little consequence. It is too painful to think.

Tasting and the ability to distinguish smells and being aware through these our own existence are like experiencing the sense of touch or that of sound. Our ability to relish food when hungry is a combined actuality of all senses. If we do not smell and see our taste may not be relishable at all. In a similar scale we experience the world in its wholeness only through a combination of all our senses. Memory is a great aid in locating ourselves within the contours of our known world. Thoughts and associated ideas also hasten to our aid in relishing the quietness of things.

Seeing is an amazing faculty that aids in our experience of the world. Our eyes are remarkable sense apparatuses that are turned outwards to a world of colour and light. Our perception of the world depends a great deal on the way we see and sense the objects and our surroundings. We make sense of things and sensations only to the extent that we are able to recognise those in terms of our sight. Seeing and believing are integrated. In many ways we can say that we are alive only when we can see around, and permit light and shade to objectify everything around us. If only our sight could also be turned inwards – a stranger sense of physicality could come to our aid in understanding as well. But then what we call seeing is that openness to light that makes everything visible through the transference through our irises and the reflection in our retinae. Here as elsewhere the operation of the nerves and brain cells also come into play. Any deviation or aberration in our perceptive faculties could lead us to see differently. Closing our eyes completely cuts out the world out there.

I have always wondered how those who are deprived of the sense of sight right from birth see things – their other four senses we are told could be more acute and thus come to their aid in this process. Nevertheless there is a certain sense of habit formation that helps these unfortunate lives to get by in terms of their perception of the world of objects and the real out there. Now, our own ways of seeing is also not much different after all. Most of the time most people do not see at all, they just see what they have been taught to see habitually. It is almost like blind people just getting by. Just because one has the physical apparatuses of eyes, nose, ears, tongue, and the tactile skin all open toward the world does not add up to the truth of being able to sense right. We see most of the time through our own familiar sense not what is there at a given time. Similar is the case with our other senses too. Our sense of fragrance and stink and the other distinguishable sensations of touch and taste likewise are certainly habituated in terms of our relations with the rest of the world. The process of learning to see and sense on one's own is indeed a challenge: of altering our perceptions. An inward turning is what is called for. The quiet world of objects and things and sensations would then begin to articulate a different truth for us. We drop our mental constructions and learn to see and sense afresh. Then the world would reach out to us. Just as we become aware of the fact that our idea of time is a unified organic concept, while our sight is a multiple factor on things and sensations as they flee us by. This is true of all our other senses – this difference between unified concept of essence and the fleeting multiple experience. Hearing, tasting, smelling, and touching – all are equally fragmented experiences unified conceptually by our notion of a sense of unity and organicity.

There are two kinds of relationships possible in our contacts with the outer world: attachment and detachment. When we engage with the world through selfless love and act accordingly we find that a living relationship can be built up from within and without ourselves. When we detach ourselves from the outer world of sensations we move in quiet over the deeps of profound inner experiences, freely. Either way a positive connection would result in genuine contact. However, as emotive beings we tend to fall in love with objects and sensations that we are intimate with, and when we pass into the next we are bitten by deep nostalgia. The second mentioned attitude of detachment is indeed a rarer one. To hold and to have to love and to cherish only momentarily and then pass without that profound tug in the heart is a rare human ability indeed! This is where the saints tread.

We know that having and being are two sides of the same stuff of life – this life appears momentarily meaningful when we have and hold, possess and cherish, everything we value. However, the moment we pass through we lose control of all we had, and sadness results. Perhaps the only way is to let go. All things pass and in silence. This is the quietness of it all. Silence is at the heart of being. Our touch, our taste, our hearing, our smelling, our sight are all *passim*, we are voyagers in space and time, and our consciousness moves as torch over everything we sense, and we pass. This is the totality of our lives. This sense of seeing and passing. And, life, *on occasion, becomes a kind of elegy for lost moods.*

We come to realise the truth of these things only when we pause at least for a split second in our mad rush to do and to have. Once we perceive this quietness of being we cease to be the same anymore. It might so happen that only in times of crises we get to see this fleeting truth of things. After all, we are such transient beings.

4
The True Voice of Raga

My father had by birth and background, a sense of sound and a sound of sense. He was far from being a musician, nevertheless his musically-sensitive ear was tuned on to the finer aspects and nuances of the Carnatic kind and he had a genuine ear. However, among his all-time favourites were often those rustic Dravidic beats and rhythms of the drums and horns and cymbals– which could probably sound like the crude cawings of the crows against a backdrop of the most elegant *swansong* of the refined Carnatic to the purist ears of the classically trained! Now, despite his love for the classical Carnatic any day, my father could also easily be swayed by the rhymes and rhythms of what now goes under the name of *folk and Dalit.* I have often watched him going into a sort of trance, eyes tightly closed and hands beating away to the non-complicated *talas* of the folk rhymes. When occasion demanded, he always played the simple tunes of the people's variety for us as children and egged us all thus toward evolving a sense of the secular and spiritual in terms of an eclectic aesthetic which he had gained, on his own.

We grew up listening to the famed renderings of the Classical maestros alongside those of the *desi* kind. Among Appa's favourites were Dandapani Desikar's cinematic rendering of Nandanar's *Ayye metha kadinam* (the lyrics of Gopala Krishna Bharathiar, done for the movie of that name), the over-dramatic versions of *Kelungal Tharappadum* (the Tamil popular song built around the life of Christ, and the A*llah, Allah*, songs by Nagore E.M. Hanifa – all ever so popular in their own times among the not-so-highly evolved or the so-called non-elitist music lovers. But, even now after many years when I listen to these, my eyes naturally overflow with the touch of the evocative and powerful feelings that these "crude" renderings proffer to any sensitive *sahrdaya.* Let us not demean them as being overly dramatic and sentimental. If very idea of music is to touch the heart, then touch they do. There is a direct rendering of emotions, a singular reaching after.

Tales of the Saivite Saint Nandanar, for instance, are popular in the Tamil country and yet so very few among us realise the subversive nature of the Tamil religio-mystic tradition – this could also be perceived in the internalisations of the Abrahamic religions in their own *bhakti* versions as well. Bhakti has so often been deemed to be mere submission for salvation. And that is how it has been projected in the popular minds, in a trivial way. In our own times after the decay of the Dravidic movement (which opposed the entire idea of religion in any form as being mere opium of the masses, and which has now petered into mere party politicking stunt for certain power-hungry politicians for their own self-seeking gains) the idea of bhakti has only gained momentum in the minds of the common people as surrender to the innumerable idols and paying obeisance to the ceremonial splendors of a dominant deity. Somewhere along the way, the Tamils appear to have forfeited the direct living link with the subversive tradition of Bhakti which survived for the most through the marvelous renderings of innumerable musicians of equally endearing compositions of great saints.

The saints of the south Indian folk tradition – the Alwars and Nayanmars, like the Kannadiga Lingayats and their Telugu counterparts – were all great composers on their own; they sang addressing their favourite deities as if directly confronting them in a language of everyday emotion and feeling and often spoke in the first person. The wonder and uniqueness of these saintly compositions reside in their ability to wheel freely in and out of joy and pain, laughter and tears, delight and sorrow, life and extinction of the senses. The *lord* that they address and most of the times even quarrel with and curse, is someone who is more of a friend philosopher and guide than any all-powerful male potentate. In almost all their impassioned compositions they find solace and comfort in the arms of their beloved deities in a sort of finality, in peace and contentment. This final identity might be achieved after the great *viraha* or pain on account of separation, or a sort of heightened existential *dukkha* – but their compositions almost always lead the listener or reader through a variety of moods and feelings which are on their own powerful enough as religious experiences.

Nandanar, Pattinathar, the other major Saivite Nayanmars and Vaishnavaite Alwar saints may not all have been composers of equally popular songs or perhaps many of their compositions were not set to music, or not even recorded for posterity. But then their *vacanas,* their statements, their utterances, their lines, have seeped into the minds of generations of listeners. The simplicity of their style and the directness of their expression certainly have something to do with this. Strangely enough this is generally true of most of the

Dravidic saints of the great Bhakthi period in south of India – despite their cultural, linguistic and psychological differences, each one embodied in their own specific idiom the experience of oneness in simple terms but never reducing anything to the simplistic level.

There is this popular tale of the 16th century Malayalam poet Poonthanam Namboothiri who composed *Njanappana* in simple Malayalam and submitted it to the well-known Sanskrit pundit and poet Melpathur Narayana Bhattathiri while he was at the renowned Guruvayur temple in Kerala, with a humble request that the greater poet might perhaps find time enough to glance through the verses. Bhattathiri in all the haughtiness of a scholar asked at once why the verses were not in Sanskrit, the accepted format for versification, and of course the language of the gods! Poonathanam replied that he was only at home in his own mother tongue, Malayalam. Bhattathiri at once dismissed the poor aspirant from his presence and the humble poet was totally shattered. He turned to his beloved Lord Krishna in complete surrender. It is said that a voice was heard from within the *sreekovil* (the sanctum sanctorum): "Poonthanam's bhakthi is closer to my heart than Bhattathiri's *vibhakthi* (grammatical inflections!)" Krishna of course is famed for his love of the simple and the passionate: and see how he dismisses the pompous and grandiloquent. The tale of course continues with Melpathur falling sick and paralytic in one heap and later recovering after becoming a penitent and repenting deeply for his haughty behavior toward the simple bhakti poet! The Lord of Guruvayur is certainly one for revealing his taste for both the high-brow and the low-brow art forms – the *marga* and the *desi*, for He is adept at appreciating the classical and the folk at one go! The language of the gods, Sanskrit and the people's lingo Malayalam, were both equally like honey to the lordly aesthete! Melpathur and Poonthanam were on the same level for the discerning eye of the Lord – albeit the openly declared love for the simple.

Telugu is a fabulously rich language – and the more rich on account of the innumerable *kritis* of Tyagabrahmom – Saint Tyagaraja. Of course there are innumerable compositions of Annamacharya and Bhadrachala Ramadas in the language only to mention two other notable saint poets. Nevertheless Tyagaraja occupies a position of uniqueness in the rich tradition of Carnatic music. Muthuswami Dikshitar, Syama Sastri and Tyagaraja constitute the Classical Trio unparalleled in the history of music elsewhere. In the Carnatic tradition there is this unique blend of the high and low art – compositions in the language of the masses like Telugu, for instance, reach into the level of high classical art, especially at the hands of a virtuoso like Tyagaraja. Sanskrit no doubt is the language of the gods but when Tyagaraja writes *yenataro mahanubhavalu anatari ki vandanamu* – (many are the great ones to them all my salutations!) the art of music reaches the heights of oneness with the great art of poetry. It has been said that he dedicated this great piece to the maestro Shadkala Govinda Marar, a renowned vocalist of his time who could render tonal variations in six *kalas*!

Sabdartha sahitau kavyam says Bhamaha, *sabda* sound, and *artha* meaning, become integrated into one, and *kavya*, poetry, is born! Music is the highest art, or in other words, *all art aspires to the condition of music* – for its directness of reach, and the richness of its dimensions. Tyagaraja is the visionary poet with an eye for music: in him *raga* and *sabda* merge into one oceanic being.

All this is possible only when the poet is the visionary – able to see Rama in all and everything. There is this amazing composition that goes like this: *moksamu galada bhuvilo jivan muktulu gaani vaaralaku*… (Is salvation attainable by anyone in this world who has not realised the Self?) Towards the end of this extraordinary piece he says: *vina vadana loludau shivamano vidha merugaru tyagaraja vinuta*. Such is the force of pure poetry! Although Tyagaraja was a devout Rama bhakta he could poetically experience the divine presence of Siva here in this ultimate poetic piece (He states: To those who cannot intuitively perceive the mind of Siva, who worships *naada* through the *Veena*, is salvation attainable?)

Siva is the supreme musician, he plays the Veena and his musical notes are supposed to wring the living hearts out – we become his music: and this is the touch of *nadabrahma*, the *alukika ananda* or divine beatitude. [According to *Muktika Upanishad*, there are only two kinds of Mukti – *'Jivan-mukti'* and *Videha mukti'* or *'Kaivalya'*. The same Upanishad also mentions 'sālōkya', 'sārūpya', 'sāmīpya' 'sāyujya' to be four types of Mukti. (*Muktika Upanishad*) Those who are familiar with Sri Aurobindo's discriminations of these states can see the similarity in perceptions here.]

In another amazing kriti Tyagaraja sings: *raga sudha rasa panamujesi, ranjillave O manasa*… (Relish in the essence of swara, raga, and nada, and be illumined O mind) Here the kavi in Tyagaraja propounds that engrossing one's own self in the raga, swara, and nada you will ultimately merge with the nature of Siva, as *Omkara nada.* This is the ultimate experience of *sangitamukti,* perhaps. To listen to the rendering of this kritis (*mokshamu galada* and *raga sudha rasa*) with all one's heart and head would be the ultimate *mukti.* The sahrdaya becomes one with *sabdabrahma.* One forgets the language of the *sahitya*– Telugu merges with the language of the gods very much like the Dravidic drums leading the soul into a crescendo of devout experience. There is the sublime in the humble, and the tiny in the true – the vast and the beautiful (*satyam, sivam, sundaram*).

One listens to the Carnatic maestro or to the folk poet with one's heart and soul. One has to have the touch of profound feelings and emotions in order to reach the divine – the experience is one where the heart and the head become fused together and then everything vanishes leaving no trace. Even those mortals among us who have not seen the face of Siva would be able to recognise and realise the divine through this composition. This is the dance of Siva in the *poyyatha ponnabalam* (the golden temple of no untruth) that Nandanar speaks about in this line *poyyatha ponnambalaththayya yirukkumitam*! (the suggestion is of course, the temple at Chidambaram – Take a closer look at this very concept where the *chit* (consciousness) merges with *ambara* or *akasa*)

There is nothing that differentiates the true aesthetic experience in the final analysis, because there is nothing that is untrue! Everything evolves in the dance of Siva and perishes in the touch of the divine. As I said earlier, the wonder and uniqueness of these saintly compositions lie in their ability to wheel freely in and out of joy and pain, laughter and tears, delight and sorrow. All emotions find their ultimate expression in the divine dance. As my father would have put it in his own characteristic fashion: *ellam onnuthan* (*everything is one!)*

After all, in more ways than one, spirituality is irreligious; the spiritual is boundless and unconditional, it is dynamic and vibrant and holds nothing sacred including the sacred. There is an old Tamil song that was quite popular at one time in my part of the world. It goes like this:

Nanda vanathil oru andi
Avan arezhu nalaka koyavanai vendi
Kondu vandan oru thondi

Athai kondadi kondadi
Pott utai thandi
Nanda vanathil oru andi

The Begging Bowl of Clay

An andi there was
In Nandavanam
Who prayed and prayed
At the potter's door
For days on end to get
A begging bowl of clay
He danced with joy
All the way back
With his begging bowl of clay
He danced with it
In sheer delight
That he dropped
His begging bowl of clay.
He broke
The begging bowl of clay…

The unconditional and uncaring manner in which the *andi* – the mendicant – drops his hard-earned begging bowl of clay in a frenzy of dancing, is the real spiritual way of being, where nothing matters any more. The breaking of the bowl is the final release into the real. Musical delirium leads one through the entire gamut of *bhavas* through to the ultimate release of the merely being human!

Emily Dickinson the American poet once confided in a letter… *If I feel physically as if the top of my head were taken off, I know that is true poetry.* This is true of music too. But the simile is not something without any experiential grounding either. The aesthesis of the raga is heard in the ear of the ear – the *srotasya srotam* – felt along the veins, distanced and integrated at once in the brain, and relished in the *hridaye guhayam* (the secret cave of the heart) – what if the deity is referred to as Siva, Vishnu, Christ or *ya Allah*? True music is the touch of the divine. And the divine is everywhere: we need to hear it with our hearts and sense it with our minds. In the aesthetic of the divine there is no high or low art – because the vertical and the horizontal emerge in a multiverse and space-time. *This is the true voice of raga.*

5

Raga Sudha Rasa and Alaukika Ananada

A little while ago, while discussing that amazing *kriti* of Tyagaraja that begins with this remarkable evocation: *raga sudha rasa panamujesi, ranjillave O manasa…* (*Relish in the essence of swara, raga, and nada, and be illumined O mind!*) I felt that I needed to dwell a little more in this context and perhaps even take a detour into the demarcations of spiritual experience that Sri Aurobindo proffers. It could be that one might strike a parallel here.

In this unique composition, the *kavi* in Tyagaraja propounds that by engrossing one's self in the Raga, Swara, and Nada one will ultimately merge with the nature of Siva, as *Omkara Nada*. Perhaps, this is the ultimate experience of *sangitamukti* or liberation through music, vouched as true experience by spiritual masters (*forgive* the gendered structure; and let us use this for want of a better sensitive word at this point)

Music as Tyagaraja states here, will bestow on one all the fruits of Sacrifices, Rituals, Tyaga, Yoga, Bhoga – in terms of the ultimate beatitude. This leads one toward the total dissolution of the little self that a genuine *bhakta* too seeks. Bhakti, one has to remember can be of various forms as evidenced by the innumerable dimensions that the pioneers of the Bhakti cult have established. Worship, with fixity of consciousness and purity of feeling and free of all extraneous thought, becomes itself a sort of *Bhavasamadhi*. As a result of this Bhavasamadhi, the Bhagavan appears before the inner eye of the bhakta, in the form which he/she has chosen for worship. The vision is not merely a matter of imagination; it is a direct experience.

Sri Ramakrishna has illustrated the two variant phases of the bhakta's attitude in terms of the monkey and the cat. The monkey's offspring clings vehemently to the mother's back or belly as the case may be – this is like the ardent bhakta who never lets go of the Bhagavan. On the other hand, like the innocent kitten allowing itself to be caught between the jaws of its mother and be lugged from place to place, the other kind of submissive bhakta surrenders himself totally to the Bhagavan. Both are devotees of the lord, both experience compassion and liberation – but there is a qualitative difference.

There are four distinct states of awareness that the bhakta passes through in terms of god-realisation and final realisation or mukti – yet these need not be in this respective manner or order: *Salokya, Samipya, Sarupya, Sayujya*

Without difference of location, when one abides in the presence of the Bhagavan, in the self-same place, it is called *Salokyamukti.*

The experience of realising all that is seen as the glory of the Bhagavan besides being always with the Lord, as in *Salokyamukthi* is referred to as *Samipyamukti.*

Existing ever with the Lord, witnessing always the glory of the Bhagavan, and becoming suffused with God-consciousness is *Sarupyamukti.*

When all traces of difference disappear, and that final onness is attained that the *Sayujyamukti* stage is reached.

This comes of only with the aid of the Divine, with what is usually understood as *Grace*. Bhakthi results also in the attainment of *Brahma Jnana*. Even if the Bhaktha does not crave for it, the Bhagavan vouchsafes it to him.

It has appeared to me that Sri Aurobindo had experienced all these four states Salokya, Samipya. Sarupya. Sayujya – poetically, as evidenced through his short poems over a period of time. His contention was that poetry works as an index of the evolving human consciousness, and his own poetic experiences were qualitative evidences of his spiritual states of awareness and becoming.

A poem titled *Trance*, composed on 15-10-1933, evidences the experience of **Salokya or abiding in the presence of the spirit.**

A naked and silver-pointed star
Floating near the halo of the moon;
A storm-rack, the pale sky's fringe and bar,
Over waters stilling into swoon.

My mind is awake in stir-less trance,
Hushed my heart, a burden of delight;
Dispelled is the senses' flicker-dance,
Mute the body aureate with light.

O star of creation pure and free,
Halo-moon of ecstasy unknown,
Storm-breath of the soul-change yet to be,
Ocean self-enraptured and alone!

The image of the star, the moon and the sky over the tranquil sea is established in stark contrast to the ... *storm-rack, the pale sky's fringe and bar* – and later interlinked to the last-but-one line – *storm-breath of the soul-change yet to be*... The poem abides in the softening presence of the spirit despite the turbulence of the inner soul. The poet writes: *My mind is awake in stir-less trance* (or is it *starless*?) This is the pure experience of *Salokya.* The experience is structured in the three stanzas of the poem – while the first stanza revolves around the star, moon, sky, and sea, the second gathers in the mind, heart, senses, and body – the third correlates the earlier two. The star of the opening line connects to the mind *awake in stir-less trance;* the moon in the next connects with the heart; the sky links up with the senses; the waters of the sea links up with the body. The star that was naked becomes pure and free in the final stanza; the moon achieves ecstasy; the sky breathes soul-change and the ocean becomes enraptured in its aloneness. All because of the experience of the nearness of the spirit, the *Salokya.*

Now, the experience of ***Samipya,*** is when the self-starts seeing with the spirit-eye. Let us take a poem composed on 18/19-9-1939, entitled, *The Self's Infinity*:

I have become what before Time I was.
A secret touch has quieted thought and sense:
All things by the agent Mind created pass
Into a void and mute magnificence.

My life is a silence grasped by timeless hands;
The world is drowned in an immortal gaze.
Naked my spirit from its vestures stands;
I am alone with my own self for space.

My heart is a center of infinity,
My body a dot in the soul's vast expanse.
All being's huge abyss wakes under me,
Once screened in a gigantic Ignorance.

A momentless immensity pure and bare,
I stretch to an eternal everywhere.

The opening line *I have become what before Time I was,* lead the reader away from the spatio-time-bound experience of the little self into the vastness of eternity. This union of the self, eternity and infinity is played out in the silence of the timeless being beyond all mutability. And this sonnet in rather conventional mode splits into the octet and the sestet at the point of intersection of the spiritual experience: *My heart is a center of infinity...* Now from what actually happens within the structure of the poetic experience is the transference of the point of vision from the mere mortal to the spiritual. The poet signals this effect in the opening sequence itself:

A secret touch has quieted thought and sense:
All things by the agent Mind created pass
Into a void and mute magnificence.

The qualitative transformation also achieves a different dimension on account of the spiritual eye and self: this is definitely the experience of *samipya* – seeing with the spirit-eye. In another poem composed almost during the same period on 17-10-1939 we can sense the similar experience of ***samipya.***

He is in me, round me, facing everywhere.
Self-walled in ego to exclude His right,
I stand upon its boundaries and stare
Into the frontiers of the Infinite.

Each finite things I see is a facade;
From its windows looks at me the Illimitable.
In vain was my prison of separate body made;
His occult presence burns in every cell.

He has become my substance and my breath;
He is my anguish and my ecstasy.
My birth is His eternity's sign, my death
A passage of His immortality.
My dumb abysses are His screened abode;
In my heart's chamber lives the unworshipped God.

17-10-1939

When the poet writes: *He has become my substance and my breath;/He is my anguish and my ecstasy*… he expresses this joy without much strain, not overburdened with words. Here we sense the presence of the human element still in terms of the experience of joy and anguish and of course that is what adds to the uniqueness of this short piece. In fact there doesn't appear to be much observable marked difference between the two states of salokya and samipya. There is only a qualitative expansion that seeps over the spiritual unity in the second stage. However, one could never state categorically that these experiences could be graded in terms of the lower and higher. Both are unique. On a similar note the next two stages of *sarupya* and *sayujya* are also to a great extent similar, with albeit slight differences in the scale of ecstasy (beatitude) and expression.

Sarupya. (becoming suffused with spirit)

All is abolished but the mute Alone.
The mind from thought released, the heart from grief,
Grow inexistent now beyond belief;

There is no I, no Nature, known-unknown.
The city, a shadow picture without tone,
Floats, quivers unreal; forms without relief
Flow, a cinema's vacant shapes; like a reef
Foundering in shoreless gulfs the world is done.

Only the illimitable Permanent
Is here. A Peace stupendous, featureless, still.
Replaces all, - what once was I, in It
A silent unnamed emptiness content
Either to fade in the Unknowable
Or thrill with the luminous seas of the Infinite.

1933-1934 Nirvana

Sayujya. when all trace of difference disappears

If perfect moments on the peak of things,
These tops of knowledge, greatness, ecstasy,
Are only moments, this too enough could be.
I have assumed the rapid flaming wings
Of souls whom the Ignorance black-robed Nature brings
And the frail littleness of mortality
Can bind not always; a high sovereignty
Makes them awhile creation's radiant kings.

These momentary upliftings of the soul
Prepare the spirit's glorious permanence.
The peace of God, a great calm immanence
Is now my being's boundless atmosphere.
All parts are gathered into a timeless whole;
All moments last in an eternal Year.

29-9-1939 & 02-10-1939 Moments

If Poetry could ever be an index of the godward journey of the evolving soul then these poems definitely can stand testimony to being such. What strikes the sahrdaya at the very outset is the genuineness and the sincerity of the poet. I have always argued that Sri Aurobindo was essentially a poet who ceaselessly attempted to capture in many poetic voices the shades of transformation that his inner self underwent. His poems are the symbolic markers in these attempts. There is very little deliberation of cerebral intervention or attempts to craft new words for newer and newer experiences. What on the other hand appears to happen is that old and used words which would normally sound frayed and discoloured due to overuse in other situations here reappear in renewed light and perhaps in their reborn states. States of being like salokya sarupya etc. are too subtle to submit themselves to ordinary expressions and only a genuine poet who is perfectly attuned to the *sound of sense* can rephrase them in different linguistic orders. Sri Aurobindo is such a type of poet who when all is said believed with all his strength in the power of words to reflect profounder levels of human experiences. For him the mantra was the ultimate solace for the evolving human mind in the ever widening dimensions of its spiritual journey. In the mantra sound and sense merge and emerge in unison. Vision, experience and expression constituted the graphic trajectory of this journey. Inspiration and expression had to occur on a similar scale. Inspiration would hasten the vision while the word made possible the expression. A choice union of vision and the word comprised the mantra. Its dimensions were aspects of both the experiential and the existential. This where what he termed integral yoga or purna yoga came in. After all, as he succinctly puts it in his *Life Divine, all life is yoga.*

Sri Aurobindo has been considered by many negative critics as being too intellectual and highbrow to be a poet at all. But then in my view he is essentially a poet who does not deliberately try to be philosophical in his writings, simply because poetry and the poetic process of god-ward becoming are both two sides of the same paper for him: tear one and you tear the other. His is poetry of the spirit and the four states of intense spiritual experience as I have tried to show are qualitatively captured in their subtle variations and shades as only a major poet could. Craft he certainly has, and as for images and words he is certainly limited on account of the unique nature of his preoccupations. Now, where words stagger under the heftiness of the expression music would step in with ease and elan. In many ways both Sri Aurobindo and Tyagaraja are attempting to capture the bliss of spiritual experience and unison. The touch of the divine alters the state of the mortal mind – words seek newer dimension of meaning and *raga* newer dimensions of *rasa.*

The question that has been tormenting me all along is how far the poet can reach before addressing that stasis of silence where words falter and fail – where pure music takes over and *Laya*, that formless quality of the force-field of the spirit becomes possible. Perhaps all art genuinely aspires to that condition of music of the *alaukika ananda*! As the poet has phrased it:

> The peace of God, a great calm immanence/
> Is now my being's boundless atmosphere.

Index

A

Academic circles, 29
Aesthetic system, 88, 107
Aesthetic theory, 11, 73, 77, 89
Ancient Indian tradition, 32, 35
Anglo-American, 31
Anglo-Germanic philological heritage, 127
Aurobindian aesthetics, 16, 86, 87
Aurobindian scheme, 38, 44, 68, 108
Aurobindian terminology, 40, 53, 89
Aurobindonians, 25, 29, 120, 123

B

Bengal National College, 13, 79
Bhagavad Gita, 25, 53
British colonialism, 10, 76
British Romantic poets, 16

C

Chronological manner, 18
Conventional scholars, 29
Coomaraswamy points, 73
Cosmic being, 21
Critical theory, 28, 32
Cultural geographers, 119

D

Dialogical engagement, 30
Divine being, 21, 23, 86
Divine transformation, 44, 46

E

Eco-aesthetic theorising, 29
Ecological criticism, 47
Eco-spiritual discourse, 38
Ecosystem culture, 31
Elemental symbolism, 32, 35, 37
English language running, 39
Environmental justice movements, 47
European classical learning, 10, 76
European Romantic tradition, 32
Evocative multidimensional map, 53

G

Geo-psychic realms, 39
Geo-psychically Indian narratives, 31, 33
Global outlook, 31
Global perspective, 9, 75
Gnostic humanity, 10, 75

God-ward experience, 108

H

Higher Mind, 53, 56, 85
Holistic transformation, 47, 72, 127
Human ecology, 35
Human nature relationship, 32, 34

I

Illumined Mind, 53, 56, 85
Indian cultural outlook, 32, 35
Indian languages, 12, 67, 79
Indian spiritual tradition, 33, 49
Indian wisdom, 10, 76
Intellectual philosophies, 80
Islamic world, 14

M

Mahakavya, 7, 41, 53, 55, 60, 61, 62, 64, 65, 69, 70
Many-sided development, 12, 78
Marxist historical materialism, 102
Militant nationalism, 10, 76
Militant nationalistic activities, 11, 77
Moksha, 34, 36
Monumental biography, 120
Multidimensional quest, 41, 53, 55
Mystic vision, 11, 77
Mystical poetry, 26

N

National identity, 10, 76
Nature interface, 30
Natyasastra, 60
Neo-Vedantic spirit, 11, 77
Nietzschean sense, 46
Non-human world, 30
Non-living creatures, 133
Notable philosopher, 11, 77

P

Phenomenal world, 17, 32, 34, 35, 44, 48, 83, 84
Philosophical exploration, 29
Philosophical insight, 10, 76
Philosophical speculations, 67, 117
Philosophical system, 44, 72
Planetary orientation, 31
Pluralism, 33
Poetic compositions, 18, 24
Poetic vision, 11, 35, 36, 40, 67, 77, 81, 94
Postindustrial culture, 31
Practical world, 30
Prodigious philosophical burden, 15
Psychological disciplines, 13, 80, 84
Purna Yoga, 72

Q

Qualitative transformation, 12, 78, 152

R

Rhythmic tongue, 23
Rig Veda, 13, 33, 37, 80, 81

S

Sensual noumena, 17

Single-minded commitment, 43, 54
Spatio-temporal interrelatedness, 33
Spiritual evolution, 19, 40, 128
Spiritual quest, 25, 72, 128
Spiritual transformation, 22, 39, 44, 53, 70, 84
Spiritualised aesthetic, 89, 108
Supra-human despair, 25
Supramental being, 40
Systematic nomenclature, 133
Systematic treatises, 39, 53

T

Tantric dimensions, 42
Tantric psychology, 85
Theoretical system, 13, 80

U

Unorthodox approach, 29
Upanishad extols, 46
Upanishadic aesthetics, 36

V

Vedic hymns, 35, 80
Vedic poetry, 15, 33, 38
Vedic temperament, 10, 76
Vedic vision, 16, 35, 67
Vital dynamism, 91

W

World-knowledge, 93, 110

Y

Yogic experience, 39, 105
Yogi-poet, 27